Farewell, Babylon

Farewell, Babylon

COMING OF AGE IN JEWISH BAGHDAD

NAIM KATTAN

Translated from the French by
Sheila Fischman

RAINCOAST BOOKS
Vancouver

Originally published as *Adieu, Babylone*, copyright © 1975, Les Éditions La Presse, Ltée, Montreal

Farewell, Babylon, translation by Sheila Fischman copyright © 2005, Raincoast Books

Raincoast Books acknowledges the ongoing financial support of the Government of Canada through The Canada Council for the Arts and the Book Publishing Industry Development Program (BPIDP); and the Government of British Columbia through the BC Arts Council.

Text design and typesetting by Teresa Bubela

NATIONAL LIBRARY OF CANADA CATALOGUING IN PUBLICATION DATA

Kattan, Naim, 1928–
[Adieu, Babylone. English]
    Farewell, Babylon / Naim Kattan ; translated from the French by Sheila Fischman.

Translation of Adieu, Babylone.
First published: Toronto: McClelland & Stewart, 1976.
ISBN 1-55192-799-3

1. Jews—Iraq—Baghdad—Fiction. I. Title. II. Title: Adieu, Babylone. English.

PS8571.A872A752 2005   C843'.54   C2005-900335-9

Raincoast Books
9050 Shaughnessy Street
Vancouver, British Columbia
Canada V6P 6E5
www.raincoast.com

At Raincoast Books we are committed to protecting the environment and to the responsible use of natural resources. We are acting on this commitment by working with suppliers and printers to phase out our use of paper produced from ancient forests. This book is one step towards that goal. It is printed on 100% ancient-forest-free paper (100% post-consumer recycled), processed chlorine- and acid-free, and supplied by New Leaf paper. It is printed with vegetable-based inks. For further information, visit our website at www.raincoast.com. We are working with Markets Initiative (www.oldgrowthfree.com) on this project.

Printed in Canada by Friesens Printing

10 9 8 7 6 5 4 3 2 1

And them that had escaped from the sword carried he away to Babylon; and they were servants to him and his sons.

II CHRONICLES 36:20

FOREWORD

W HEN I WROTE this book, the Jewish community of Baghdad, though very small, still existed to some degree. Today, there are practically no Jews left in Iraq. The prisoners of Nebuchadnezzar have left a country where they had lived for twenty-five centuries. They were there before the Christians or the Muslims. To preserve the Book, they studied it, composing the Babylonian Talmud. And while they became integrated into a series of empires, caliphates and colonial powers, they remained Jews. After years of harassment, the Iraqi government allowed Jews to leave the country in 1951, on condition that they relinquish their nationality and their property. The State of Israel, born three years earlier, took in the majority. Others took refuge in London, New York, and elsewhere in Europe and America.

Founded by the first Abbassidian caliphs, Baghdad was a great capital, an important centre of power and culture which was proclaimed "the City of Peace." Even recently, ethnic and religious minorities lived there side by side: Arabs, Kurds, Jews, Christians, Chaldeans and Armenians, Shia and Sunni Muslims. In their private lives these communities did not mingle, meeting only at work and gathering in neighbourhoods with boundaries recognized by all parties. The equilibrium — fragile and precarious and imposed by foreigners, Ottoman or British, who acted as arbiters — sometimes succumbed to tensions or conflict.

I left the city of my birth more than fifty years ago and I have never returned. It still feeds my memory and determines part of my way of being. Three years ago, this book was translated into Arabic. What a shock to read myself in my mother tongue! I have written more than thirty books in French, the language that has become mine and with which I struggle every day, like any writer. Reading myself in translation, I could sense that Arabic is still alive somewhere deep down inside me, even when I measure the distance that separates me from it.

Often, on television, I see Iraqi exiles, Arabs or Kurds, seeking refuge in order to survive. There are nearly four million of us around the world. The Jews were the first to leave. I was lucky enough to leave Baghdad in 1947, thanks to a scholarship from the French government to study at the Sorbonne. In 1952 I visited my family in a *maabara*, an encampment in Israel. The condition of the refugee is never easy, even if a country welcomes him or her with open arms. Those Jews are now part of Israel.

Today when I visit the Babylonian or Assyrian galleries in the Louvre, the British Museum, the Pergamon Museum in Berlin or the Royal Ontario Museum in Toronto, I relive my childhood excursions to Babylon and Nineveh. So many civilizations blossomed in that country! The traces they have left are richer and more meaningful than all the oil wells. And I think to myself: what a waste! A country that cannot hold on to all of its citizens!

Farewell, Babylon is not a work of nostalgia, nor is it one of resentment. I remind myself that peoples outlive their lands, even lands that are hostile. Sometimes ungrateful people damage the legacy and the wealth of their land. I never forget that Abraham was born at Ur in Chaldea, not far from Baghdad. He is still the father of all the monotheistic religions, even if his message is handled roughly. His word endures, even when we do not hear it. That is his victory; it is also our hope.

NAIM KATTAN,

MONTREAL, NOVEMBER 2004

ONE

THE COFFEE POT had just gone around again and we were all holding cups of bitter coffee when Nessim made his entrance. His gestures were emphatic and exaggerated like those of a retired actor, but he put such elation into his words that he never gave the impression of being on stage.

The discussion was lively that evening. Nazar could not contain his enthusiasm since he had started reading the American novelists. He urged the group to enroll in the school of Saroyan and Hemingway. "It's the ideal every young Iraqi writer should be aiming at."

Zaki interrupted. He disagreed with Nazar. It was in our own rich past, in the great Arabic literary tradition, that we should seek our inspiration.

"But the Arabs haven't produced any novelists," said Nazar, who had just published a collection of short stories.

"What about the *Thousand and One Nights?*"

"All right, but those are folktales that aren't really part of the literary tradition ..."

"Don't wear yourself out, we know the rest," Nessim interjected. He had written an essay on Balzac and translated several of Maupassant's stories. "Here are the models to follow."

We got together at the Yassine Café every evening, making plans for the future based on our day's reading. It was an endless debate that we resumed night after night. We were painfully tracing our path, each of us seeking in the others' approval a confirmation of the dictates of his temperament; and under cover of discussing the future of our culture, we were defending our own first writing.

That evening was marked by an unusual note. Nessim spoke in the Jewish dialect. We were the only Jews in the group. All the others, except for a Chaldean and an Armenian, were Muslim and their dialect served as our common language. In Iraq the presence of a single Muslim in a group was enough for his dialect to be imposed. But was it a true dialect? Every religious community had its manner of speaking. All of us — Jews, Christians or Muslims — spoke Arabic. We had been neighbours for centuries. Our accents, certain words, were our distinguishing marks. Why did the Christians draw out certain words? We were told that in this way they were perpetuating the traces of their Nordic origin. But then the Nordic Muslims, those from Mosul, should have spoken like Christians. The Jewish manner of speaking was sprinkled with Hebrew words, explained by long familiarity with the Bible and prayers. But how to explain the presence of Turkish and Persian words in our dialect? We would have had greater contact with invaders and pilgrims than the Bedouins. Then what about the Muslims who, during the Ottoman era, were forced to learn not Arabic, but Turkish in school?

We had only to open our mouths to reveal our identity. The emblem of our origins was inscribed in our speech. We were Jew, Christian and Muslim, from Baghdad, Masrah or Mosul. We had a common language, that of the Muslims of the region. An inexhaustible source of confusion and cruel ridicule.

What better entertainment for a young Muslim than listening to an old Jewish woman from the poor section of Abou Sifain speaking to some Muslim official? She mispronounces several Jewish words, following them with a couple of common Muslim expressions. With many contortions of the mouth, she finally succeeds only in mispronouncing her own dialect. The effect is inevitably comic.

Semi-literate Jews always studded their phrases with one or two Muslim terms when they spoke to other Jews. Borrowing a few words from the Muslims proved that one had dealings with them, that one associated with them and that one was not content with the poor company of other Jews. The rich Jews were no less ashamed of their accent and they never missed the chance to slip a few words of English or French into their conversation. A child who called his father "papa" or "daddy" was already guaranteed a future aristocracy.

The Muslims borrowed only from literary language. They felt no need to cast an unfavourable judgement on their dialect. And they turned to the dialects of Jews and Christians only to amuse visitors. A typically Jewish word in the mouth of a Muslim was synonymous with ridicule. In emancipated intellectual circles there was no thought of borrowing the Jewish accent and even less of making fun of it.

It was unusual, then, for Nessim to speak in his own accent among so many Muslims. Was it another joke? No, he was not speaking exclusively to me. He was completely free to do so, despite the presence of the others. But he was not addressing me. He was not even looking at me. He was speaking to Nazar, Said and the others.

It was very important not to attach too much importance to this new whim. Everyone tacitly wanted to attribute this outburst of comic dialect to Nessim's bantering nature. It was of no consequence. Most of all, we must guard against giving any special import to this jesting.

Nessim persisted, straight-faced. It was as though he were taking special care to choose all the Jewish words that usually got a laugh from Muslims. Imperturbably, he pleaded Balzac's case and talked of his enthusiasm for Stendhal, whom he had just discovered. Like a coward, I chose silence. Still displaying all his enthusiasm for the French novel, Nessim called on me to participate. Finally he asked me a question directly. It was useless for me to escape. He would persist.

I chose a middle course. My words were neither those of the Jews nor the Muslims. I spoke in literary Arabic, the Arabic of the Koran. Then, in a supercilious tone and with contained anger, Nessim corrected me: "You mean …" And he translated into perfect Jewish dialect. He compressed his lips in a gesture of hatred. He exaggerated our accent. I could see in his look a mixture of sorrow and commiseration. I was betraying him. I was ashamed to utter in the presence of others the words of intimacy, of home, of friendship. Nessim was forcing me to take a stand against the solidarity of the group. I could not reject our common language without humiliating myself. It was no longer the language of friendship, but of the clan. I listened to myself and the Jewish words stood out in all their strangeness, coldly naked. My sentences were frozen. Before I uttered them, I heard them echo in my ears. I was reciting a lesson I had learned. I slipped in a French word. Nessim, pitiless censor, immediately translated into the Jewish dialect.

No one smiled. The new rules of the game had been accepted by common accord. The Muslims with good grace paid no special attention to the new language that was stating its unaccustomed presence. Generally they looked at us without seeing us. Now, mysteriously, they recognized our features. They were noting a new colour in the panoply. Later, everything would be restored to order, as no one would want to admit the existence of particular cases.

In our group we were neither Jew nor Muslim. We were Iraqis, concerned about the future of our country and consequently the future of each one of us. Except that the Muslims felt more Iraqi than the others. It was no use for us to say to them, "This is our land and we have been here for twenty-five centuries." We had been there first, but they were not convinced. We were different. Was our colouring not lighter than the Bedouins? Did we not know foreign languages? The fact that the best students in Arabic in the final examinations were Jews, that the Alliance Israélite school produced the best Arabic grammarians, changed nothing. Our identity was tainted. So be it. Nessim was assuming this difference. He wanted it admitted. He did not intend to convince and he had no evidence to produce. He was presenting a fact. We were Jews and we weren't ashamed of it.

By the end of the evening, we had won the game. For the first time the Muslims were listening to us with respect. We were worthy of our dialect. We were clothed in our own garments. Our mouths were restored to their true form, the one they had worn for generations in the secrecy of the home. This was the likeness which best suited us and it was reabsorbed in the intimacy of our minds. We had not been forcibly assimilated into some vaguely defined group. We had not been cast in a mould with unknown rough surfaces. The masks had fallen. We stood there in our luminous and fragile difference. And it was neither a sign of humiliation nor a symbol of ridicule. In a pure Jewish dialect we made our plans for the future of Iraqi culture.

We did not take shelter behind the veil of an artificial equality. Our features were emerging from the shadow; they were being drawn. They were unique. Our faces were uncovered, recognized at last.

In the heat of the discussion, Janil and Said borrowed some of our familiar expressions. They stammered over words they had heard so often but never allowed to cross their lips. They apologized for their awkwardness.

As the evening progressed, Jewish words came more frequently to these foreign mouths. It was decidedly uncomfortable to carry on a long conversation in two distinct languages. Perhaps Nessim would stop being so intransigent. Now it was up to us to go along with the others, go halfway towards those who displayed such obvious goodwill. It was particularly important not to claim victory too soon. We had to hold on to the end. New habits are created so quickly, and so quickly forgotten. Nessim's tenacity bore fruit. By the end of the evening Said and Janil and all the others too were being introduced to the Jewish dialect, with as much awkwardness as comedy in the serious matter that it was.

TWO

OUR RELATIONSHIPS with the group were steeped in quietude. We were dealing with emancipated liberals and revolutionaries who were working to demolish the walls put up by prejudice and misunderstanding.

A few darts fluttered across this limpid horizon now and then, bringing us back to order. We rejected their stigmata and soon ignored our wounds. They were merely scratches on our self-respect. We must be unbiased, must consign to oblivion these bitter reminders, these anachronistic survivors of a distant time when nothing interfered with an open display of prejudice. It was our duty to lift the veil. A few explanations, some judiciously recommended reading, and our companions' eyes would be opened, finally and forever. And then the light would shine in all its brilliance.

It was an exchange which Nessim and I pursued for hours at a time. To chase away his perpetual concerns, I made a show of imperturbable optimism. I minimized the meaning of certain words and gestures while Nessim saw in them undeniable signs of terror.

I often had to yield to his arguments and give in to the evidence. When he reproached me for not speaking about the position Chaplin had taken against anti-Semitism in my article on him, I had to admit that I had, in fact, devoted several paragraphs to the question that was so painful for both of us, that I had even quoted the words Chaplin had put into the mouth of his hero at the end of *The Great Dictator.* Said, going beyond his role as editor-in-chief, had taken it on himself to eliminate these paragraphs. He would not have mentioned it if I hadn't asked him for an explanation. There was nothing unexpected in his reply — something about the layout. Nessim accused him of hypocrisy and I tried feebly to contradict him. Fundamentally, we were in perfect agreement. And a year later Said would no longer be concealing his game. One day when I didn't come to the café, his pan-Arabic orthodoxy was confirmed. He announced to the assembled group that he would carefully censor my writing, which often concealed a strong odour of Zionism.

Nessim and I shared the same prognostics, the same reading of the events, but I had the hesitant desire, despite the present opposition, to hope for better times and to go on believing in a cooperation which would be essential but difficult to achieve. Far from reproaching Nessim for his intransigence, I urged him on. And so the balance was restored. On the risky road where I was adventuring, he was my security and my keeper.

Nessim carefully read the works of all the great playwrights, Greek, French or English, contemporary or classic, although he had never set foot in a theatre. He suffered from a fever like the one that had afflicted his models, and in a few days he had completed a tragedy with contemporary resonances. But his characters bore Hellenic patronyms. It was a harmless exercise, as there were no stages in Baghdad. If no one knew whether the work was playable or not, the author at least had the satisfaction of self-respect; it would be submitted to the judgement of readers.

Its imminent publication had already been announced in the newspapers. Out of prudence and a simple concern for phonetics, the editor felt it necessary to Islamize Nessim's family name, and Abraham became Ibrahim. What was the difference? It was the same patriarch, the father of Isaac and Ishmael, whose story is told in the Bible and the Koran. But it was harder to fool Nessim. He was a Jew and it was as a Jew that he would introduce himself to the public. Abraham's face would not be disguised under the anonymity of Ibrahim, and the author's stubbornness would definitely frustrate the few dozen eventual readers of this Graeco-Judaeo-Iraqi work.

Nessim forced his nature and spent all his time throttling his most powerful impulses. Fearing his true spontaneity, he flaunted a borrowed one: hair always in a mess, a shirt never burdened by a necktie and exposing most of his chest to the wind. He took great care with his untidiness, but he was only concealing his natural elegance. He did his utmost to hide his tenderness behind an apparent inflexibility and cruelty, but he only presented an air of insolence that was hardly amusing. He walked quickly, and during our long walks I was forced to adopt his rhythm. It was as though we were in a race. He hurried on, driven by an urgent need to move. And then he would be led imperceptibly to unmask his flayed features, to strip bare his own raw wound, which he was bound to protect from the cruel looks of strangers. He took nothing seriously and discovered the comic in the most dramatic situations; but one had only to touch, unconsciously, this secret cord and he would be transformed into stone.

On the threshold of this invisible door he would stop short, frozen. The scene that unwound before his child's eyes rose out of the shadows in all its nakedness and violence. Who among us was not marked by the *Farhoud?*

For centuries we had taken pride in living on good terms with the Muslims. Then in just one night thirteen centuries of shared life and neighbourliness crumbled like a structure of mud and sand.

Farhoud. It was the beginning of May. The hot summer wind had been blowing for several weeks and we had already moved our beds onto the roof. We were asleep when the signal was given. Baghdad was a free city and the Bedouins could make a clean sweep.

We had lived through a month of martial fever and nationalist talk. That year, 1941, the British army was retreating on all fronts but it was resisting in the face of assaults by the Iraqi forces. There was no breach in their line of defence at Habbaniyah, and the Union Jack still flew at the Shouaiyba base. Morning, noon and night, communiqués from Iraqi headquarters announced hypothetical victories and added up the enemy's heavy losses. The government of Rashid Ali was growing impatient. The help he was anxiously awaiting from Berlin was long in coming. Hitler made promises and did not keep them. Between a communiqué and a vengeful declaration, the radio broadcast endless messages in code addressed to friendly countries, to allies near or far. In this holy war being fought against a reviled invader, there was no question of Jews or Muslims. We were all in the same brigade in this fight to the death against a colonial power that was sucking our blood and our oil.

On the threshold of puberty, I was being tortured by the violence of nascent desire. What better diversion than this noble struggle in which we were recklessly hurling ourselves? We would liberate our country. Jews or Muslims, we had but one enemy: the English. The Englishman would be crushed. And with help from Germany we would be rid of him once and for all. The tall blond Germans were mythical figures, valiant saviours of wounded honour. Before the Muslims' overwhelming enthusiasm we kept silent, but in the intimacy of our homes it was another story. My brother, my uncle, our neighbours, spoke of the Germans in low voices and cautiously, as of an imminent catastrophe. We knew how Hitler would treat the Jews, and the Nazis' Iraqi disciples did not reserve a more enviable fate for us. But I did not share these old people's fears. There was no possible comparison between Iraqis and Germans. Once we were independent, we would all work together, united in our desire to build a new society.

Suddenly the news broadcasts on the radio became chaotic, infrequent. The Iraqi army was continuing its victorious march. Its triumphs were increasing but it was storming the base at Habbaniyah where the British forces were fighting with their backs to the wall.

Two days before the end of this war, we were visiting neighbours who had a powerful radio that picked up the Arabic broadcast from London. We strained our ears for the latest news transmitted by the enemy. A summary of collapses, retreats, withdrawal before Hitler's invincible army. The one exception was Iraq, where the British had finally won out over the insurgents.

The next day there was a new commotion. Six German aviators had landed in Baghdad bearing living witness to the solidarity of the German government and to its support in the noble mission of the Iraqi nationalists. All day long, strolling down Rashid Street, they put on their show. Passersby would touch their arms, their backs, their shoulders. Some, more daring, would seize their hands and kiss them, as though the soldier were a venerable religious man or a powerful tribal chief. Veiled women threw themselves to the ground before these blond messengers, kissing their feet, a sign of submission and servitude no man would permit himself, despite the universal fervour.

But the aviators' visit was ephemeral, like a flash of lightning. These representatives of distant allies had come too late. They recorded a report of defeat and prepared an account of the wreckage.

We learned of the rout on the radio. The masters of the airwaves had suddenly changed their tone. The chiefs had abandoned the crew to its fate, then left the country. The British soldiers found themselves at the gate of the city. The young king, accompanied by the regent and a few faithful ministers, left their hiding place in Iran and returned to the palace. Between the departure of the one group and the arrival of the other, there was a pause. The city was left to itself. This absence of a guiding authority opened the floodgates to an unbridled, chaotic march. A wind of impunity was blowing. And it took just one hour to stir up a sleeping, pent-up people. The Bedouins had heard the signal and they were prepared. Instinct was the law. All was permitted. They had come back to ancient celebrations. Henceforth it would be the tribe that ruled. In all the neighbouring villages, in the makeshift suburbs, the nomads left their campsites. The abandoned city was theirs. It was offered to their cupidity, long unsatiated. The entire city? No. All the tribes would be saved but one. It was the law of the desert. The Jews would bear the cost of this repressed hunger, this devouring thirst. Two days and a night. We could hear shots in the distance. They came closer and gradually grew clearer. The conflagration invaded new grounds. Soon it would swallow up everything.

They advanced. Armed with picks, daggers, sometimes with rifles, they unfurled in waves, surrounded the city, beleaguered it. Rallying cries crackled on all sides. As they passed through, they brought along Muslims, spared the Christians. Only the Jews were being pursued. As they advanced, their ranks swelled, teeming with women, children, and adolescents who ululated as they did on great occasions such as weddings and feasts. They reached the target. It was the poorest part of town, Abou Sifain. They pushed down the gates and moved in. What could not be carried away was demolished. Then a second wave entered the devastated site. The men were sent away. Those who put up the slightest resistance had their throats cut on the spot. And the women were made to submit to the will of the men. Despite their cries, the Jewish women were beautiful. They were dirty, dressed in rags. They smelled of rancid fat and babies' pee. They were good animals.

The commotion spilled over into new neighbourhoods. Where there were no jewels or money, the invaders took boxes of clothing and furniture. Often faithful and loyal wives came to take turns with their husbands. On their work-hardened shoulders, one would place a sewing machine, another a chair.

After Abou Sifain, Hennuni. Now they were cleaning out the houses of Taht el Takya. A brief respite followed, time to carry away the spoils. On the outskirts of town, tents were swollen with mirrors, dishes and clothing. They caught their breath and prepared to set off again, for new conquests. The ranks dispersed. They hesitated. Reached the forbidden limits. First, the mixed neighbourhoods. At the Shorja bazaar, Muslim fruit vendors and Jewish spice merchants were neighbours. How to decide between the closed shops? They went along Akd el Nasarah, the Christians' street. They crossed it. On Rashid Street a battalion began to break down the iron gates. There too were many Muslims and some of the shops suffered the common fate. They crossed Bab el Sheikh, a Muslim stronghold. Slowed down at Sunak, a neighbourhood shared by Jews and Christians. They reached the threshold of Bab el Sharki. There, hesitation, questions and doubt would end. The neighbourhood was entirely Jewish.

In the last ten or fifteen years an entire Baghdad suburb had been populated by Jews. An advance party of families promoted to wealth had transformed what had been a place for pastoral walks into a seething community. Beyond Bab el Sharki, streets took shape one after another. They were broad, bordered with eucalyptus, paved and clean. The houses rose up along Bustan el Khass (the lettuce garden). On sunny Saturdays when I was a child, my father would take me for walks in this enormous vegetable garden. We went along the furrows, crossing the paths that had been specially cut for the tourists who came out of the city's entrails. None of the walkers would think of depriving himself of a freshly picked lettuce. All along the paths, merchants sat behind mounds of vegetables carefully arranged in a circle, discussing with their customers the price for one or a dozen. We washed our sandy lettuces in a public fountain or under the tap in one of the open-air cafés that enclosed the Bustan el Khass.

On one of our walks, I noticed that surveyors were measuring the furrows. My father explained that streets and houses would soon erase our Saturday countryside from the map. The garden was divided into lots and families were starting to leave the muddy alleys and move into small houses. Symbol of wealth and modern times, each lawn was adorned with roses, jasmine, an orange tree or an apple tree.

In a few years the suburb, now named Battawiyeen, extended beyond Bustan el Khass, which was soon only a memory.

The first synagogue in the district was dedicated to the memory of a merchant who had died without leaving any children and bequeathed part of his fortune to charity. As the streets had no names, the synagogue served as a landmark. We lived two or three streets to the east or west of the synagogue.

Some families were so modern as to have chosen European

architecture for their new houses, so that the interior courtyard disappeared. But the roof was invariably flat, for in the summer modernists and traditionalists alike all went to sleep on the roof.

The wave of violence was reaching this district. The *Farhoud* had every appearance of a tribal engagement. With one difference: the attacked tribe was unarmed, ignorant of the tradition of such combats, surprised in its confidence and fear. It could not defend itself. Once the torment had passed, high deeds of bravery and heroism erased from our faces the shameful marks of fear and defeat. With a hail of pebbles and bottles, women and children stopped the forced and terrifying march of battalions of murderers and plunderers.

Those of us who lived in the Battawiyeen waited, on the watch for the slightest noise. We were the supreme target. In these broad streets, no resistance was possible. Nor did anyone think of it. We kept our ears cocked. According to my father, the shots were diminishing. But no, they had only changed direction, my uncle said. And my mother expressed the hope of all of us: that it was the English firing against the Bedouins. They would not delay their entry to the city and they would deliver us.

We put off going to bed, for then we had to climb up on the roof where there was nothing to stave off our terror or our anguish. Finally, my mother took the lead.

The evening wind usually brought us snatches of songs and music from some open-air cabaret. But this night was torn by cries, the howling of a mass burning with thirst. With one voice it proclaimed the sharing of the spoils. Suddenly chiefs appeared from everywhere, organizing the attack, giving the signal.

We were alone. Automatically we all squeezed onto the edge of a single bed, huddling against one another. My father, who did not often force upon us his role as head of the house, on this evening became our guide and our shield. He knew all the psalms by heart, and began to recite them in a voice that was trembling, dry, monotonous. We tried to follow him, to whisper some of the words. But the screams of the hunters drowned our uncertain voices. They came closer, and it was my mother who whispered, "Let's go down."

Stopping on the stairs, we clung to one another. My sister was asleep. There was no reason to awaken her.

On this evening my father, who had never been able to do justice to the melody of the psalms, did not even pretend to sing. He managed to extract the words, and we clung to every one. Each line bore the weight of a heavy secret, of a message of deliverance. Were we invoking God or did we simply want to lay low our enemy, disarm our misery, put off the terrifying rendezvous? We were waiting patiently, whiling away our time. The hour would come eventually. There was nothing to do. Most important, we must not think about it. We were of the psalmist's tribe. We prayed in Hebrew. The Bedouins are so unlike us. For hundreds of years they had buried themselves in the infinity of the desert, but now from the depths of the ages they were moving towards us. From now on nothing would belong to us, not even our lives.

I had barely glimpsed the richness of life and now it was going to be snatched away from me, forever. I had never made love, and I was going to die without experiencing something I dreamed of constantly. All the beautiful women I could have touched, held, discovered.

Now the sound of gunshots came to us from farther and farther away, and at the first light of dawn we dozed off, pressed against one another, leaning against the walls, crouched on the steps.

Our sleep was interrupted as we touched, seeking assurance. Half awake, I glimpsed my mother, passive now, given up to sleep, her mouth open. With all my strength I wanted to disappear into unconsciousness, lose myself in a long tunnel that would be impermeable to the sound of shots and crying.

The sun was already blazing when my mother shook me: "Get up and go lie downstairs."

And so I slept. I did nothing but sleep. Could it have been only a bad dream? I felt light. I was still alive. But I was afraid to let go, to believe in it entirely. Perhaps it was too soon.

In the evening we learned that the Iraqi army was making its entrance and that it already controlled the streets of the city. A Kurdish soldier, responsible for protecting us, was dispatched to our street. A messenger from the world of the living. The sentinel chose our house for his observation post because it was situated in the middle of the street. He knocked on our door and asked for a chair. We rushed to anticipate his desires. Was he thirsty? Hot? Hungry? The neighbours across the street offered him cool lemonade. The next-door neighbours' maid brought him a plate of sliced cucumber.

In other circumstances we would have found his pronounced Kurdish accent comical; but the fact that the person who was defending us against our aggressors was himself a Bedouin could only instill confidence in us. His Kurdish accent became a sign of affinity in the face of a common enemy, and for the first time we found it charming. At that moment we would have found unsuspected beauty in the language of the Kurdish street cleaners.

Whatever hesitation we might have felt about believing in our deliverance, after the next morning we could no longer ignore the fact that the roads had been opened and the hordes of plunderers had withdrawn. In the poor parts of the lower town, at Hennuni and Abou Sifain, those who had been robbed and looted, new orphans and old widows set out in dozens, in hundreds, towards the rich neighbourhoods, knocking on the doors of the houses that had been spared. We had lost nothing, while the others had lost the little they possessed. They came to us for a reckoning, not charity or alms, but sharing; and one did not offer them leftovers or half-rotten fruit.

"Now that we can go out, we have to go to the fruit seller," my mother said.

My father came back with enormous supplies of cucumbers and apples.

"Here's all that was left. The stores are being cleaned out quickly," he said. "Perhaps tomorrow I'll go to the market."

For days, victims came knocking at our door. The apples and cucumbers were arranged in the entry. We learned, a little at a time, what had happened to each street, each neighbourhood. Accounts of horror were followed by descriptions of acts of heroism. A hail of broken bottles had stopped the wave in front of the synagogue. And Taht el Takya where our cousins lived? And Akouliya? And Aadhamiyah, my paternal grandmother's neighbourhood?

THREE

THE CHIEF RABBI published a notice of mourning: the community had lost three hundred members. People laughed in his face. Only three hundred! Was he in league with the government? Or perhaps he only wanted to lessen the horror.

The dead were entitled to a prayer and the repose of their souls. And what of the hundreds of girls who had been savagely raped? At best they hoped to keep their misfortune secret.

Order was restored. A large depository was set up at the Shamash School and those who had been plundered went there to recover their property. The police went to the Bedouins' tents and to certain Muslim neighbourhoods to collect any furniture that was too cumbersome to be carried to the depository.

Two weeks after the events, the fever of war had passed. I explored the city again, saw that it was marked by its wounds. At the start of the war of liberation, the signs on the stores had been hastily whitewashed. All those who had displayed their modernism with Latin characters printed above their Arabic names had erased with a brush stroke the mark of colonization. No businessman wanted to leave any doubt about how he felt towards the language of the imperialist enemy. Some, more obviously contaminated by the foreigners, repudiated their presence even more radically. The London Restaurant was renamed the National Restaurant and the Café Piccadilly gave way to the Café Mosul. Jews and Christians, sometimes even sooner than their Muslim competitors, were also quick to lift the veil of the imperialist shame that concealed the noble origins of our beloved capital. But soon all the signs would be repainted. The English words would be reinstated as hastily as they had been erased.

Fearfully I crossed every street as though there might be land mines. Would we ever know? Perhaps there were still some places where the rule of law had not been restored. A new city, a strange one. And yet the streets still seemed familiar. In the heart of the nightmare, I dreamed of it. The houses were still standing. My school was in its proper place. I had to have the courage to pick up the thread where I had dropped it and tell myself that the horror had been only a momentary halt. We would have to begin again.

I didn't dare go to Nessim's house. I was paralyzed by fear. He lived near our school, the Alliance, and his street had not been spared.

When we met again, we looked at one another, bewildered and happy. We were men and we could not allow our tears to flow. We were embarrassed; our words stuck in our throats. He told me what was happening to our classmates: as far as he knew, none had perished, but many had been plundered. Nothing much had happened to Nessim — only his uncle had been murdered!

When the pillagers had broken into his house, his uncle had refused to be a passive spectator as they removed his possessions. The vandals had tried to push him out of their way. He persisted, insisting on annoying them. He insulted them, told them to get out of his house. He called for help. In other circumstances, these actions might have been effective, but this was the *Farhoud*.

They pushed him into the bathroom, held him down, stretched him out on the floor and slit his throat, like a sheep. His aunt talked about it constantly, adding new details every time she told the story of the murder. Nessim had not been there but he kept reliving it in his imagination.

"As soon as the laws and controls are relaxed, the Muslims will rediscover their slaughterers' souls," he said.

For months he thought he could recognize in every Muslim in the street the face of his uncle's murderer.

FOUR

WITH THE RESTORATION of order, the Jews came out of their numbness and stupor and began to plan for the future. Leaving the country headed the list.

Every morning hundreds of families besieged the passport office. In the first days we witnessed great changes in customs and habits. Perhaps the tide of savagery had had some beneficial consequences: the Muslims had finally become aware of the blind corruption that undermined the administration and touched everyone, from messengers to ministers. The policemen greeted us and did not hold out their hands. Messengers announced our presence to their masters without expecting any payment. Besides, our tips had never been generous. Had we really made up our minds to leave, or were we simply showing the authorities what we were thinking? If they didn't want any more of us, we would go immediately, leave the place and abandon the Bedouins to their fate.

For those who had firmly resolved to carry out their plans, there was another question: Go away, but where?

Germany had just declared war on Soviet Russia. Hitler's armies were erupting all over Europe. It was reassuring to know that the Führer's Iraqi disciples were behind bars, but the Nazi forces still had all their military strength, and their hatred of the Jews remained intact. Under these conditions, it would have been an aberration to throw ourselves into the lion's den.

America? Impossible. Once you had all the documents, you had to wait years for a visa you would probably never use because a civilian passenger would be unlikely to find a place on a boat.

Every morning the family went to the passport office as soon as it was open. We were all there, my mother's mother, my unmarried uncle, both of whom shared our house, my parents, my sister and brother. My mother soon realized that her presence was not indispensable, especially since she could no longer neglect her cooking and household tasks.

Then her questions became precise, pertinent, embarrassing. What safe harbour had we chosen? My father, in turn, gave up his daily walk and rushed back to his work as an official in the post office. For my brother, my sister and me, it was a diversion at the start of the long school holiday.

Every morning we were there, on time. We passed through every stage: police inquiry, testimony as to the authenticity of our Iraqi birth. An army of professional witnesses offered their services. Middle-aged men blocked the streets beside the passport office. We bargained over the price of a testimony and then went to the official who recorded, under oath, the affidavit of these men who were seeing us for the first time, who swore that they had seen us born. Officials closed their eyes to certain anomalies. The man who declared officially that he had been present at my father's birth was ten years younger than him.

During the long hours of waiting, the little courtyard, edged with trees and rose bushes, served as a café. In the shade of orange trees, on those hot days the cool breeze lent a note of reality to our unexpected welcome by the officials whose offices surrounded the courtyard.

We all met there: neighbours, former neighbours, cousins, classmates, colleagues. Before entering into an account of our immediate or distant plans, we began by describing what had happened to us during the days of the *Farhoud*. In this passport office we became aware of our place in the world. We had cousins in Indonesia who were claiming us, brothers in Calcutta who offered their hospitality, uncles who had made their fortune in Mandalay and were now inviting us to share their prosperity. And like titles of nobility, we recited our prospects for new lives.

"And you, where are you going?"

With many variations, the reply was always the same.

"I'm going to my uncle in Shanghai."

"With the whole family?"

"I'll go by myself first, to prepare the way. My parents and sisters will come afterwards. How about you?"

"I'm going to my uncle in Tehran," I said. "My older brother will go first, as a scout."

Each of us named a close or distant relative who had suddenly become the link that connected him to the free world.

FIVE

THE DAY AFTER the *Farhoud* we cabled my uncle, telling him we had escaped unharmed. Later we sent him letters, keeping him informed of our progress in the passport office. His invitation was a long time coming. Would Tehran be any more secure? The question must have been asked by every person who attempted to leave a country whose emperor made no secret of his pro-German feelings.

The story of our distant uncle was part of the mythology of my childhood. His success had gained him the stature of an omnipotent giant. My mother used to tell me stories as a reward for good behaviour. Among my three favourites was the legend of Dungur Khushayban, a superman who overcame numerous obstacles and was constantly running into others, even more challenging. He finally delivered the woman he loved from the hands of the evil bandits. And Dungur himself was overwhelmed by fate, by luck and love. I always dreaded the moment when Dungur would conquer the seven mountains and cross the seven rivers, but it was his ordeal by fire that filled me with terror. Through the flames that would devour him, Dungur could see the face of his beloved. As my mother neared the end of his trials, my disappointment would grow. Then I'd ask her questions, making her repeat certain episodes, putting off the end of the story.

"Tell me the one about Joseph now," I would beg.

"Tomorrow."

The adventures of Yossef al Siddik were something like a family chronicle. Yossef was the name of my grandfather who, like his ancestor, had named two of his sons Manasseh and Ephraim. When my grandfather died, my mother and my uncles were dispossessed, stripped of their inheritance. My mother was only ten at the time. Encouraged by the example of our biblical ancestor, my uncle, who was barely sixteen, set off on his adventures. Once he made his fortune he would forgive all the wrongs inflicted on him by his half-brothers. His ordeals were many and my mother had an endless store of anecdotes about his courage and the strength of his soul. He never forgot his sister, never deprived her of his affection. She was poor, but her love for her more fortunate brother was never altered by envy or jealousy. And while everyone feared and flattered him, she felt no need to demonstrate her pride or admiration. She was convinced that he owed nothing to chance but had snatched everything from an adverse fate. When she told me I resembled my uncle, I knew this was a great benediction, her highest praise.

When her brother was sixteen, he did not want to answer the call of the Ottoman government. Jews were put into the battalions destined for Siberia and subsequently became the scapegoats for any defeats or retreats. And so he did not wait for his call. Furnished with only his intelligence and his will to conquer, he set off on the long road that led from Baghdad to Hamadan. Many times he was nearly murdered. Luckily he was gifted with exceptional eloquence. He knew how to win people's confidence and friendship. He managed to disarm the worst barbarians, with only his kindness and his words to defend him. On foot or on mule-back, having finally completed the rough crossing, my uncle contemplated the skies of Persia. He worked without pause, his ardour erasing any distinction between day and night, and fortune smiled on him.

More than any legend, the story of my uncle fed my imagination. It was the promise of distant and fabulous lands where merit would triumph over all constraints and where we, calling on our own resources, would demonstrate our valour, give proof of our courage and apply the gifts of our intelligence. In our ancient city we assured the rearguards of uncles, cousins, brothers and nephews who had given in to a mysterious and powerful desire and had snatched jealously guarded treasures from fate. Their loyalty was unshakable, their fidelity unfailing. We were their true and only homeland and they overwhelmed us with gifts and money. Sometimes distant cousins, long forgotten, emerged from the shadows as if to test our own loyalty. These wandering sons had been able to resist the adventures to be found on a road strewn with unknown scents, strange women and sumptuous palaces. I remember our excitement when a treasure was discovered. My father told us the news one afternoon when he came home from the office. A lawyer, my mother's cousin, was trying to locate all the members of our large family. A distant cousin had died in Java. No one had even been aware of his existence. He had left a fortune and no direct heir. He had died a bachelor, because once his fortune was made he had never returned to his birthplace to look for a mate. In low voices, one episode was mentioned: all his life this illustrious cousin had shared the bed of a Japanese woman. He had not, however, taken it upon himself to give her his name. We had only scanty details about the kind of business he had set up overseas. It was whispered that there was nothing honourable about it, that he made his money by selling opium and by white slavery. Other voices were raised in his defence. Our cousin had never forgotten his family. In our eyes, this should be enough to redeem him. He had specified in his will that his property was to go to members of his family, to the fifth degree. Were we in that group? My mother was sure we were but the only proof she had was that our family tree had a strong trunk with few branches. My grandmother was lost in conjecture. Was the prodigal son the child of Sarah, of Rivka, of Khatoun or of Habiba?

SIX

BEFORE WE MOVED to the new Battawiyeen suburb, we had lived in the old neighbourhood near the Meir Synagogue. Our house was across from the *alawi*, the wheat, corn and rice storehouses. In summer we moved our beds to the roof and a white iron enclosure provided privacy from glances of passersby. Small holes at the top let us look out on the street without being seen. Often at sunset, before I got into bed, I would spy through these openings on the muffled throbbing of the outside world. Once a week the Bedouins would come with their camels. They would sit them down just across from our house and feed the animals as they unburdened them of sacks of grain. Where did they come from, these vigorous men with their chiselled faces, who conversed with their camels with the familiarity reserved for humans? Very ugly animals, with their small heads, jaws in constant motion, their humps and their bodies covered with enormous callouses.

I would beg my mother to lift me above the enclosure. Speaking to the closest Bedouin, I would shout with the secret satisfaction of crossing boundaries that adults would not have the audacity to transgress: "*Ammi, Ammi.* Uncle, Uncle."

The respect I owed to every older man required me to use this familial term. In these circumstances, it tasted of the forbidden.

In the Muslim dialect, I would address the stranger. The tall Bedouin would spin around his *akal* and turn his head. Trembling with fear and courage, I would toss off, in my best Muslim dialect, "May God help you." And the man, still talking to his camel, would answer, "May God keep you, my son." And so he became my uncle and I his son. In the world of childhood, I was neither Jew nor Muslim, and without running any risk I could speak directly to a Bedouin.

LIVING ON THE FRINGE of the Muslim world, we could sense its strangeness, which was often transmuted into exoticism. For us it was also a world of hostility and compromise. We were close to the Muslims and consequently it was imperative that we avoid their blows, appeal to their goodwill. As long as they left us alone.

When a Jewish mother reprimanded her son, she would call him a Muslim. The Muslim mother returned the insult by calling her offending son a Jew.

My paternal grandmother was skilled at manipulating her power. She lived with my unmarried uncle in the suburb of Aadhamiyah, a predominantly Muslim district. Here and there a stray Jewish family was crowded into the end of a street in this cluster of Shiites and Sunnis. Often the bus that took us there made a detour to Kadhimayn, a sacred place for the Shias. In the distance we could see the gilded mosque, which was considered the most beautiful in the country and, it was said, in all the countries of Islam. We would get off the bus in front of another mosque, more modern but no less impressive.

I often went with my father to visit his mother. We would go along the street where the mosque stood and cross the covered market, a cool and salutary pause in the summer months. We came to the path edged with gardens before passing the palaces where our most distinguished citizens lived. Through the grille came the scent of roses and jasmine that perfumed the garden of Rashid Ali, who had declared war on Great Britain in 1941. Moved by a childish veneration, I would slow down, forcing my father to linger with me before the great house of the poet Al Zahawi. We finally came to the few Jewish houses stuck between the river, the palaces and the gardens.

My grandmother enjoyed great prestige among the wives of the more eminent citizens and their servants. In everyone's eyes, she was "the doctor's mother." She relentlessly lavished advice and remedies and she had drugs to take care of irritated eyes, upset stomachs and stiff backs. No one was concerned about her medical competence, even less that of my uncle. He dreamed of one day becoming a doctor but meanwhile he worked as a laboratory technician. A trifling distinction. Did he not work in a hospital and wear a white smock, even at home? Was he not a great English doctor's right-hand man? My grandmother never missed the chance to take advantage of all these titles. Besides, it would have been the height of ingratitude to question the goodness and knowledge of a woman who offered her remedies and advice and never asked for anything in return. People received care without having to move or see a doctor, without spending the day in hospital corridors. My uncle did not interfere with his mother's growing prestige; on the contrary, he often came home from the hospital laden with potions and pills which she would judiciously distribute.

It was only partly true that my grandmother received nothing in return for her generosity. I was in a good position to know. The gardeners used to open the grilles of their masters' gardens for us. I was set loose among the oranges, blackberries and apples. I could pick as much as I wanted. My grandmother, though, warned me about the demon of greed. When the prohibition was removed, stripping the trees soon became a tiring game that lost its attraction in favour of walks along paths that gave off the perfume of orange blossoms. The overpowering sun on the street seemed like the memory of a distant world. And every time our teacher of Tanakh reminded us that the Garden of Eden described in Genesis was situated in Iraq, my mind drifted through my grandmother's gardens.

I must have been ten when she made me promise to be good for a whole week. As a reward, she would take me to a great celebration at the home of some Muslim friends.

The ceremony took place on the other shore of the river Tigris. My grandmother could bring just two grandchildren and my brother and I were the privileged ones. We got into my uncle's boat to cross the river. He rowed, not suffering anyone else to touch what he called, with a smile, his ship. The other shore, inhabited entirely by Muslims, had always seemed unreal to me and I had never thought I would set foot on it. I held my grand-mother's hand tight for reassurance. My admiration for her was boundless. She was powerful with all the esteem of the Muslims; and the marks of respect, of deference even, with which they received her made her grow in my eyes.

We followed the dozens of families who were rushing towards the house of one of the leading citizens. Two of his sons, aged seven and nine, were being circumcised. He had invited the whole neigh-bourhood to the feast. His neighbours, servants and relatives could take advantage of the great event to have their sons circumcised free.

Drums were throbbing. Orchestras strolled through the streets announcing the news to the world. Finally the fateful hour arrived. The children came out of the tent which had been put up specially, surrounded by their parents, holding in their hands their wounded, painful manhood. The rhythm of the drums grew and the children's cries were drowned in the uproar. It was a time for happiness and joy. When the passage of a child into adulthood was announced, all cries of pain were buried in an outburst of gaiety. From the depths of their kitchens, the women, busy all day preparing the meal for the guests, let out their strident cries.

At nightfall, rugs were spread all along the street and table-cloths laid over them. Two rows of men took their places around the tablecloths, separated by steaming meats and enormous platters of rice and fruits.

Our hosts had not pushed their hospitality to the point of inviting us to appreciate a huge variety of dishes. Besides, my grandmother, terrified as she was by the sly and frightening behaviour of the germs my uncle was always talking about, would never have allowed me to put my hand into the plates from which the dozens of guests took their portions of stuffed mutton and rice with oil.

These customs were quite unlike our own. Circumcised eight days after our birth, we had no memory of our bleeding manhood. However, we participated without hesitation in the joy, because any such outburst, no matter how strange its reasons, invited the spectator to share.

I remember another spectacle, the *Sbaya*, with terror. There is a reason for Jews to describe the *Sbaya* as a scene of horror and savagery.

Some distant cousins of my father lived in the Shia section, a rare thing for Jews. The *Sbaya*, the Muslim "passion," took place before their windows. Every year they shared their privileged vantage point with about thirty friends and cousins. My mother was prepared to miss the show so as not to expose me to need-less fear, but my grandmother reassured her: I would be fast asleep before the procession had even started.

All the shutters were closed except for a small crack that did not let in any light. No one outside must suspect that they were being observed by curious eyes. We pressed our heads against the edge of the shutters so that we could view the spectacle. We did not say a word, afraid of our own whispers. Above all, we must not offend the excited crowd, which could easily attack any sacrilegious spectators. I was afraid of the diabolical possibilities of this human wave and I dreaded what my own eyes might see. I resisted the nightmare and struggled to prevent it from taking hold of me. Tomorrow I would be walking on this earth that was being transformed before my eyes into a Gehenna bursting from the depths of time. This unleashing would be indelibly imprinted on my mind unless I did not eventually repulse its images and phantoms. I can still see the bare-chested men, panting in the chains that bound their arms and legs, waiting open-mouthed for a drop of water to quench their thirst, unbearable but sought and accepted. They flagellated themselves and inflicted as many blows on themselves as on their companions. They were reliving the slow death of Hassan and Hussein, martyrs for the faith. There were even more men armed with swords and daggers. The unfurling of the apparatus of war and of a panoply of green-and-black banners attested to the passage of death — so that the faith might triumph and live. I crouched down in bewilderment. I was convinced that the slightest gesture would signal my presence to that multitude of demons. I closed my eyes in an attempt to banish the spectacle, to exile it into an unreal domain. My mother, wanting to assure herself that my curiosity had finally been overcome by sleep, murmured my name. I did not reply. Could not the utterance of my name reach the ears of the armed men, bearers of black banners! The dramatic game, the ritual of total release — was it not the precursor of the *Farhoud*?

SEVEN

THE MUSLIM FEAST DAYS were holidays for my father, a civil servant, and all the schools, including the Jewish ones, were closed. If Saturday, our Sabbath, was more solemn for our whole population than Friday, the official day of rest, it was on Yom Kippur that our community made the full weight of its presence felt in the city.

Several days before the fast, my mother would clean the rope-and-canvas espadrilles my father wore on that one day. It would have been imprudent to wear leather shoes which might break some twig or leaf, threatening the absolute rest of this holy day. On Saturday we could have an electric light that had been turned on all night, but on the Day of Atonement when we came back from the synagogue we looked for our beds in the dark.

My mother's mother went to the synagogue with the first light of dawn. Before she left, she would waken everyone and then go ahead of us so that she could save seats for my mother and sister. For several years my brother had not even made a pretence of going to the synagogue. At first I used to go with my mother through the passages reserved for women. Then when I was older, I was entitled to sit with the men and I spent the whole day beside my father.

The entire city involuntarily observed our solemn day. With the exception of the theatre whose Muslim owner presented only Egyptian productions, all the movie houses were closed. Rashid Street, the city's main artery, was practically deserted. Muslim passersby would affect an air of nonchalance that made Baghdad look like an orphaned city. Christian and Muslim businessmen, behind their counters, seemed only to half believe in their work. In the textile bazaar, Shia shopkeepers gossiped with their neighbours as they puffed on their *nargilehs*, waiting for their rare customers. The Muslims themselves waited until the next day to do their shopping. When the Jewish stores were open, there would be a greater choice. The Jews' presence was even more evident because they were concentrated in the vibrant heart of the city. The Muslims, who made up four-fifths of the population, were scattered from Bab el Sheikh to Karkh, from Heyderkhana to Karradah, clustered between the Shias and the Sunnis.

Invisible boundaries separated the poor neighbourhoods in the Jewish community from the others. Crossing the barrier made one realize one's own wealth in comparison with the inhabitants of Hennuni and Abou Sifain, who were crowded five and six into one room. About the children of these sections I knew only the legendary image of rudeness and bad language I was warned against.

The well-to-do only ventured into these tortuous streets when they were looking for a maid or a laundry woman. One day I went there with my mother when she wanted to replace the Kurdish laundry woman who came to our house every two weeks. We went from one foul-smelling alley to another, looking for the place where Kurdish Jews who had emigrated from the north usually flocked together. The Kurds, the most deprived of the Jews, supplied the community with people to do the heavy work: porters, furniture movers, laundry women and maids. Huddled together in their sordid neighbourhood, they lived on the margin of the community.

Each neighbourhood had its own hierarchies and was distinguished by those families with illustrious names who lived there; except for the poor sections, which stagnated in anonymity.

We knew even less about the Muslim sections. To go downtown we crossed Bab el Sheikh. We always preferred to go by bus, circling the great mosque. It was a forbidden part of the city and my mother had never crossed it on foot except when she was forced to do so, trembling with fear and uncertainty.

For my grandmother it would have been unthinkable to enter the Muslim section. Besides her fear of the unknown, she did not want to open the way to a possible reciprocity and allow Muslims to have a place in the synagogue.

When I was eight or nine, an emergency brought me to the heart of a Muslim stronghold. I had wrenched my elbow while playing leapfrog. That evening my father took me to see the rabbi of the neighbourhood synagogue who was also a bonesetter. He rubbed my arm and my forearm after coating them liberally with sesame oil. He bandaged me and blessed me. The next day my elbow hurt even more. Even though it questioned the *hakham*'s talents as a bonesetter, my mother took me to see him again. My elbow was hurting more and more.

Then neighbours advised my parents to have the afflicted limb seen by a miracle man, a Muslim café owner in Bab el Sheikh. Nothing could resist his power — neither a broken leg nor a sprained arm. My mother covered my head to hide my fair hair from Muslim eyes. When she dressed me, she took every precaution to disguise my Jewish origin. Holding my father's hand, I felt as though I were leaving on a trip, and secretly prepared myself to cross the boundaries of my own country. How surprised I was when I entered these foreign alleys to see doors that looked like ours, windows that were identical to those on our own houses. And the fruit sellers and spice merchants were just like those in Battawiyeen and Dhorja. They wore the same headdresses, the same *akals* and *arakchines* as other Muslims. When my father asked passersby for directions to Haj Alwan's café, he murmured in his best Muslim dialect. He could not deceive anyone about the nature of his own language, but our passage aroused only indifference. The people we questioned were neither kind nor ill-tempered. I had expected that we would be taken for curious creatures, that people would stop and look at us, that they would hurl insults or even throw stones at us. So we were not so different from the others after all.

From the outside there was nothing unique about Haj Alwan's café. The same benches, the same matting and tables, the same music and games of backgammon. Haj Alwan was a devotee of Zewar Khana, the Persian gymnast, and he had outfitted his basement for athletics. I watched young people jumping, shouting and responding to the exhortations of enthusiastic spectators. We waited until the session was over to introduce ourselves to the man in charge. There was nothing remarkable about Haj Alwan. A café owner like dozens of others. Humbly my father presented our request. I was embarrassed to hear him, a man, using this begging tone. He told the café owner of the misfortune which had befallen us and of our need for his kindness and help. Haj Alwan did not waver. He asked me to undo the bandage. I was trembling with fear and could not hold back my tears.

"Don't be afraid, my son," he said.

He gripped my hand and pulled it brusquely, with a tap on my arm. He repeated this three or four times. I could hear my bones crack.

"It's all right now. Put back the bandage."

My father, in a low voice, urged me to kiss the hand of the Haj.

"Am I all better?" I spoke directly to Haj Alwan.

"It's all right now. Come back and see me next week."

My father thanked him profusely as we hurried outside. Apprehensive and thinking about the next visit, I asked my father, "Don't you pay him?"

My father pulled my hand, indicating that I should be quiet.

"You must never talk about money in front of a man like Haj Alwan," he explained. "That would be a very serious insult."

It was quite natural for our local *hakham* to look after me without asking for any remuneration. But for a café owner from Bab el Sheikh to spend the necessary time without even asking me my name was incomprehensible. My father was content to repeat, "It isn't done. You don't pay a man like Haj Alwan."

He was exasperated by my lack of comprehension and no doubt by his own as well.

EIGHT

I F INVISIBLE BOUNDARIES isolated each group within its neighbourhood, streets and houses, it was quite different in the world of work. My father, my uncle and, later, my brother were civil servants and all their fellow workers were Muslims or Christians; but when the offices closed and each one returned to his own neighbourhood and his own people, they became strangers again.

Most Jews worked at crafts specific to towns that were leaving behind their primitive conditions. They were blacksmiths, carpenters, shoemakers, spice merchants, fruit sellers, and businessmen of all kinds. There were many clerks and low-level officials. We placed a high value on office work and the sorriest-looking individual in charge of documents enjoyed more prestige than any manual labourer.

Of course we had our rich and our poor. The most deprived were the household servants of the privileged. We had our own contingent of beggars, who were part of our daily décor. On the street that I took to go to school, I recognized each one of them. They had their reserved places at the entry to a house, beside a shop, at the bend of an alley and — most of all — at the doors of the synagogue. Near examination time we played hide-and-seek with the future and, hoping for good luck, willingly unburdened ourselves of our pocket money, giving up treats and boiled turnips. One of us would set his sights on a one-eyed beggar, another on a cripple. If our intermediary with fate too often lacked effectiveness, we would throw ourselves on the mercy of a replacement.

The marriage brokers were the barometer of society. They established salary scales and decided which trades and professions enjoyed the greatest prestige. For a beautiful girl, young and of good family, the ideal man was traditionally a businessman. Gradually the latter would find himself in competition with doctors, engineers and lawyers. Then shopkeepers, small businessmen and civil servants entered the race for beautiful young girls of good family.

The Jews were the backbone and sinews of the Iraqi state. They played this role unwillingly, in self-defence. When the British army first entered Baghdad, in 1917, forcing the Ottomans into their last retrenchment, their main concern had been to announce to the Arab population that the hour of liberation had sounded, the hour of independence was near. They needed interpreters to call out the good news and only the Jews could respond to their need.

The schools of the Alliance Israélite Universelle, established some twenty years earlier by French Jews in order to bring the light of the West to their co-religionists in backward countries, had prepared my father and my uncles for the new tasks created by the change of régime and the new master. They were among the first candidates for the privileged posts of interpreters for the British army. If the ideas of the English and French languages with which they had been inculcated in school were highly inadequate, the British officers had no choice in this land of want. They made much of these rare links with the natives, reserving for them the treatment due to the indispensable collaborators that they were.

When Iraq became independent several years later and was establishing its government service, it called on its loyal Jewish citizens, experienced now in the secrets of the civil service because of their period of probation with the "English." The post office, the railways, the customs, finance, all were overflowing with Jews. The change of régime was nothing less than brutal. In spite of the presence of Iraqi ministers and directors-general, orders and important decisions were always inspired by former British military men who had moved on to serve the independent Iraqi state as advisors. The new administration demanded that all its servants, with the exception of foreign advisors, know the new official language of the country, Arabic. Jews and Muslims set out to relearn a language which they had spoken only in the degraded form of a dialect. Turkish, an idiom they had learned in school, had automatically become superfluous. People went back to school with enthusiasm and a covetous desire to improve their Arabic for more important jobs. There were recalcitrants, of course, including my father. He considered it humiliating for the head of a family of four to go back to school.

"I have children to bring up and I can't waste time learning my own language, the one I've spoken since I was born."

The Iraqi government gave schools in the Jewish community complete freedom to teach Biblical Hebrew and foreign languages, on condition that priority be given to the curriculum of the Department of Education. All the schools had acceded to these new directives without hesitation. With the rise of Arab nationalism, the authorities became increasingly demanding. And to ensure that no subversive influence would contaminate our minds, Muslim teachers were imposed on the Jewish schools, appointed by the Ministry of Education to teach us history and how to be good citizens.

My Arab Muslim history teacher was a Kurd who made no secret of his deep sympathy for us. As the Jews were not, like the Arabs, conducting a masked war against the Kurds, he presumed on our friendship and understanding. What a mistake. We made fun of his Kurdish accent and his way of stammering the Arabic words. As soon as he came into the classroom, we gave the signal to make an infernal din. We did not even listen to him when he declared, his voice trembling with emotion, that Iraq should be proud of its Jewish children. We barely followed him when he sang the praises of the Finance Minister in the first Iraqi cabinet. He was a Jew, and it was he who had negotiated the first oil agreement with the British. "What a genius!" exclaimed our teacher, trying desperately to cover with his voice our own blindness towards one of our gallant sons. He had demanded that rents be paid not in pounds sterling but in gold. His British interlocutors misunderstood the whims of the natives and had acceded to his request. Now all Iraqis were harvesting the fruits of this minister whose clairvoyance exceeded that of all the British advisors. The price of gold having doubled in relation to the pound, we received twice what we would have obtained without the genius of our representative.

The government acknowledged the Jews' superiority in one area: their knowledge of foreign languages. The teaching of English was compulsory in all the schools in the country but it was in the Jewish schools that it was taught most effectively. In spite of such natural aptitudes, it was not our knowledge of English or French of which we were most proud, but our skill in Arabic. At the final examinations set by the Ministry of Education for students in all the schools, the first prize was invariably won by a Jew.

Our community supplied a strong contingent of translators and writers to the editorial offices of the daily and weekly newspapers. Like their Muslim and Christian colleagues, they churned out long columns of patriotic prose and homilies addressed to the royal family.

NINE

I OFTEN WENT TO the cloth market with my mother. We would
walk along Rashid Street until we came to the lanes lined
with the stalls of dozens of merchants selling velvets, brocades
and silks. I managed to decipher the multiform calligraphy deco-
rating the signs on the big stores and shops on Rashid Street, and
by piercing their mystery, I learned all the names by heart. The
Jewish tailor, the Armenian dentist, the Muslim photographer
were accidental neighbours; each had come from his own neighbourhood, his own fortified village, to clasp one another's hand
in the perpetual round of religions and forms of worship and left
in my mind a lasting image of this seething artery. Haroun al
Rashid, the great Caliph of Baghdad, proudly bore the name of
the brother of Moses, and like a cry of hope and a challenge cast
at fate, he bore the descriptive name Wise Man.

General Maude's entry at the head of the British army heralded
the beginning of a new era for Baghdad. Family records were
always dated in relation to this event: someone was born a year
after the General's arrival, another was married two years before
his appearance. My father often spoke of the Ottoman epoch, not
because it was a happy time but because it was the time of his childhood. The legendary years were those that followed Maude's entry.

For all Iraqis — Muslims, Jews or Christians — it was a golden age. Now they had an administration and a capital. This autonomous power outlined each person's future. The government was careful to prepare for the relief of the British soldiers, now advisors, by awarding scholarships for study abroad to the most deserving. In return, it only required them to put at the service of the state the knowledge acquired in Europe or America.

My father noted with detachment the love my brother and I devoted to Arabic. He often felt the need to point out his own mastery of Turkish, occasionally translating a word or phrase in this now useless language. It was his way of apologizing for his limited knowledge of the complexities of Arabic grammar.

The majority of Jews, with insatiable thirst and constant alacrity, drew on the sources of this new culture. My uncle subscribed to the Egyptian periodical *Al Hilal*; and every week my brother happily showed off the latest issue of *Al Hassid*, a weekly literary magazine founded and directed by a group of young Jews nourished on Hebraic and western culture who had decided to be the first builders of the new Iraqi culture.

Their eagerness to take their place in the ranks was not always well rewarded. At times of great enthusiasm, the Jews cherished a dream they sometimes took for fact: the new wind would bring equal hope for all. The signs on Rashid Street blazed proudly with Jewish patronyms. Our presence there, composed of many individual presences, was the result of diligent effort. The Jewish merchants' names were firmly attached; behind their windows, shirt-makers, jewellers and booksellers were not tied to the name of one tribe or the mark of one denomination.

The dice had been loaded because the state could intervene and the laws of the majority made a mockery of minority rights. For a Jew to assume the position of Director-General of the Post

Office or the Railways, he would have to prove beyond any doubt that he was indispensable, that no Muslim could replace him. Notwithstanding the country's needs, the doors of the army and the diplomatic service were strictly closed to us.

Every year our chances dwindled and the screws were put on our prospects for the future. My uncle was enraged when he was refused admission to the Faculty of Medicine. The heroic years when all candidates were welcomed with open arms were over. Now only two Jews were admitted. Wealthy parents, wanting to avoid their sons losing a year, no longer even risked having them apply to the Faculty at Baghdad. They sent them to Lebanon or Europe.

In the face of these realities, the Jews' enthusiasm for the new government gradually dimmed. Irritation, anger and disappointment grew. We were well aware that Islam was the official state religion. We learned painfully that our participation in building our country was required only where it was seen to be indispensable.

We had pitched our tents on this land from time immemorial and all down the centuries we had served the hard apprenticeship of injustice, so that we now considered it to be part of the nature of things. Was this not the price one had to pay for being different? In that respect we had no reason to envy the Assyrians, the Armenians or the Kurds, not even the Christians or Shias. We were living in the shadow of a wild beast which for years had kept a leaden silence; now, suddenly, its giant's body was stricken with fever. We could feel the jolts that shook it and then it was swooping down with all its might on one victim or another.

We belonged to tribes and each in turn was the victim of fate. Like the others, we led a double life; but more than the others, we were exposed to our neighbours' looks, because our campsites were always located right in town. No one expected us to change. No group, no government, dreamed of depriving us of loyalties or our past. One is born Shia, Armenian or Jew and one dies Shia, Armenian or Jew. Our origins had more to do with geography than beliefs. In this conglomeration, each of us possessed his territory which extended beyond walls and visible boundaries. We strolled side by side down the main street without ever blending into fraternity or anonymity.

We were Jews. We knew it. Everyone knew it. But we were also children of this land, children of the country. And that was something we had to shout, constantly cry out, for fear it would be forgotten and that we would be deprived of our share of the wealth which God had bestowed on this kingdom, his own.

Were we not the best Arab grammarians? We were pleased to quote the master linguists: a Carmelite Father, a Jewish school-teacher. It was perfectly natural. No affectation, no calculation, in the love we felt for the language we had spoken from birth, which belonged to us as much as it did to the desert Bedouins.

The names the Jews gave their children demonstrated their powerful gift for adapting to changing realities without sacrificing their old loyalties, all the while remaining unshakable in their rootedness.

In this periodically devastated land, this land of nomads, there were some examples of constancy and continuity. They had survived invaders from powerful empires. With each new master, they had to make pledges and pay a tribute in order to safeguard their heritage, avoid the threat of disappearance. Over the centuries they had been witnesses to victories and defeats, euphoria and rage. Many times they had won their rights to this land. And they were doubly its sons. Did not each of them have at least two given names? A Jewish one recalling the memory of a dead ancestor:

Heskeil, Abraham, Nessim, Ezra or Elijah, Leah, Rivka, Simcha or Rachel.

Each period added other names to these unvarying ones, changing according to circumstances, recalling the presence of the outside world which was superimposed on the eternal universe. Persian names like Khatoun were followed by Turkish patronyms like Gourdji. Then the West left its mark, with names like Flora, Regina, Renée, Albert, Edward and Maurice. New masters, new names. In their secular wisdom, mothers anticipated the rising nationalism, decking their newborn infants in ambiguous names which, at decisive times like admission to college or an office, would leave some doubt as to what group they belonged to. It would have been sacrilegious to borrow the names of Muslim saints and martyrs. No family would ever have the audacity to call a son Mohammed or a daughter Fatima. But aside from the fact that Youssef was briskly transformed into Youssuf, and Abraham into Ibrahim, names like Sabih, Akram, Zaki or Jamil increased. No religious allusion. Parents merely guessed at the character of their offspring by describing them for the rest of their lives as "generous" or "handsome."

Over the years these subterfuges ceased to open university doors. Influence and bribes made it possible for certain privileged people to fill the places reserved for Jews in the learned quotas conceded to them by the officials of the Ministry of Education. After the Faculty of Medicine, it was the Ecole Polytechnique and then the Faculty of Pharmacy which excluded them. Only one refuge was left: the Faculty of Law, a catch-all where no one was refused and courses were given night and day to future lawyers and politicians. Each official seeking a promotion rushed off to the registration office in this factory for turning out men of law. Slim consolation for the Jewish candidate, rejected everywhere else.

Would he be a civil servant? His chances were shrinking. Politics? No use even thinking of it. Such an occupation was good only for the sons of sheiks and ambitious citizens who were not afraid to take risks. Between a Jew and a Muslim, even a Shia, the political battle would be underway with weapons so unequal that it would be lost for the Jew from the outset.

A university diploma would be better than nothing. One would accept what was still accessible to him. The Jews studied law with the vague feeling of efforts expended in vain. The exceptions were rare. This was the case of my brother who studied law because he liked it.

Education was our only weapon and we would not let ourselves be stripped of it. Young Jews had to be able to go abroad to study, and parents who had the means did not wait for the community's sanction.

TEN

SOMETIMES WE WENT to visit cousins who lived across from the office of the Community Council. Then I would see the *hakham* Bachi, the Chief Rabbi, going into his office. His ritual costume and long beard gave him the appearance of a Jewish sheik. On grand occasions, at coronations or investitures, he represented us with dignity and he seemed not at all out of place beside the *imam* and the patriarch.

His way of conducting the community's affairs was not appreciated by everyone. I observed a stormy demonstration that took place in front of the *hakham*'s windows the day after the Community Council elections. They were protesting an increase in the price of kosher meat. Like their predecessors, the newly elected members had decided to give the monopoly on the sale of this meat to the highest bidder. The concessionaire would pay a certain amount to the Council to cover the administrative costs of the community services. It was an indirect tax to finance the Council, paid by those who ate kosher meat — and that included almost all the Jews.

The concessionaire was almost always a Muslim. No Jew would voluntarily lay himself open to the anger of the whole community, which every year grumbled at the increased price of meat — that is, against the rise in taxes.

My maternal uncle, very active in community work, looked with great disfavour on these demonstrations whose instigators were always recruited from the less fortunate members of the community.

"All they have to do is stop eating meat if they aren't happy," he would say cuttingly.

He spent two evenings a week at the Meir Hospital, where he was secretary-general. An honorary post, of course, which was the pride not only of my uncle but of my grandmother as well. For this son, an uncorruptible high official, was not rich. His community responsibilities raised him up to the same level as the leading members of the community and he sat next to generous donors and wealthy businessmen. The latter took pity on him. It seemed confounding to them that he would put so much zeal into the service of a state which was undermined by corruption and ungrateful to honest men.

As many Muslims as Jews used the community's health and welfare services. There were a general hospital, a clinic for eye diseases and a school for deaf mutes. Wealthy members of the community on whom fortune had smiled in other lands financed these institutions, reminding family and friends of their loyalty to this land. The majority of these faithful migrants built synagogues and schools. Because of them and those who had not had to expatriate themselves to make their fortune, the community found itself endowed with a network of primary and secondary schools which could receive the great majority of Jewish children. The Anglo-Jewish Association and particularly the Alliance Israélite Universelle helped raise the level of these institutions, which enjoyed a good reputation among the Muslims.

The public schools opened their doors to Jews and Christians as well as Muslims, without restriction. But for the Jewish or

Christian child, sharing a desk with a Muslim was like a long voyage to a foreign land. And most parents preferred to barricade themselves behind the walls of their own neighbourhood. Of course the outside world still had its attractions, on condition that it was decked out in the prestige of the West. Many Jewish and Muslim families sent their children to the schools run by the Soeurs de la Présentation or the American Jesuit College. Bringing together children of various faiths, accepted and desired by the parents, did not promote intimacy. They were unshakable in their desire to avoid one another.

Social boundaries were no less obvious than those marked by religious differences. Among the Jews, the Alliance schools were the meeting place of the privileged classes, even though the school's administration admitted a few poor children, paying their expenses. Often the poor parents were the most reluctant to send their children to the same school as the descendants of the great families. Other considerations were at stake too. What language would be chosen, aside from Arabic, of course? Future rabbis huddled together in the Midrash and small rabbinical schools. At the Alliance we learned four languages: Arabic, French, Hebrew and English, with emphasis on the first two. At the Shamash School, English was supreme and pupils were prepared for the British matriculation at the same time as the examinations of the Iraqi Ministry of Education.

Alone among the others, the Alliance schools received foreign teachers, mostly Greeks or North Americans, because of the headquarters in Paris.

ELEVEN

W E HAD GREETED the return to school with sighs of relief. A lot of water had gone under the bridge since the *Farhoud*. We had passports, and that took the place of revenge. We could leave now. Some had gone to join relatives in India or Persia, the only countries that were accessible. They were few in number. The others, not knowing where to go, had wisely stored the precious document in a drawer.

The new government had put certain insurgents on trial as an example, choosing them at random, and hanged some of them in the town square. The Jews greeted this display of strength and goodwill enthusiastically. It reassured them. The presence of the British army in the heart of town restored our confidence. These soldiers, who were fighting the Jews' mortal enemy on other fronts, revived our hopes and our feeling of security. And there was lots of work, enough for everyone. My brother had just finished his legal studies and foresaw a shining future. My mother thought I was too restless. The remedy: next year I could look for a job. While I waited, I had to keep busy and spare my mother the extra trouble of looking after me. My brother knew his power over me. I would have done the most thankless tasks in return for his approval. There was nothing particularly exciting about the program he had organized for my vacation: to learn by heart the *Moallakat*, the works that pre-Islamic poets had hung along the walls of the pagan temple of Al Kaaba, which Mohammed turned into a religious sanctuary. As I memorized the lines, I made it a strict rule to learn the meaning of the unusual words whose mystery my brother would decipher for me by the hour. For my own pleasure I read translations of the novels of the French writer Michel Zévaco. The translator's name, Tanios Abdouh, was printed in larger type than the author's. However, the author's name was always preceded by the words "the celebrated" or "the great French writer." How disappointed I was when I learned later from my French teacher that there was nothing famous about this "celebrated French writer."

When we went back to school, I was armed with new words. This pre-Islamic heritage was truly mine. The face of the world was changing and we would not have to expatriate ourselves. For the Russians were in the game now. A few years of patience and the world would be transformed and our enemies laid low by the new defenders of our freedom. We would no longer need to leave Baghdad.

I was not the only one who felt the accelerated rhythm of our days. When we met in the main schoolyard, we had one longing: to say that we were no longer the same, that even if the torment had not touched us directly, affected our families or fortunes, it had nonetheless transformed us, fashioning our souls and our thoughts forever. We were going to forge new forms of action.

A week after school had started, I learned of a secret society. Cells were being organized in each class under the direction of a student in his final year. The members were taught how to handle weapons, were inculcated with the heroic deeds scattered through Jewish history and given a broader knowledge of modern Hebrew. The goal of the organization was to form self-defence troops.

Nessim had a foreboding and he joined spontaneously. If I hesitated, it was largely because I mistrusted the suppliers of revolvers who sought protection in anonymity. My abstention was intolerable to Nessim, who was burning with a blind fever. It was a painful test of our friendship. We barely spoke to one another. I was quite willing to be convinced but he did not allow me to question his enthusiasm. During recreation periods he would go into a crowd, haranguing the recalcitrant, galvanizing the faithful. He looked at me. I had to take sides or give my reason for not joining. I stood in the midst of several friends and as I spoke to them I painfully sought reassurance. I was opposed to the secret society, that destroyer of friendships. It changed our affinities and the dictates of our hearts. It introduced new elements into our lives: blind obedience to unknown leaders, suspicion, denunciation.

Clandestinity had some irresistible attractions. It gave our games a sudden unfamiliar gravity and weight. We were discovering an unsuspected power. Nessim was the leader of a cell, and that only reinforced my hostility towards the society.

Feeling excluded, I came upon secret meetings and conversations unexpectedly. Assignations, mysterious meetings, were happening behind my back. And Nessim was going his own way. He was an author now. He edited a news bulletin and an ideological program directed at his troops. He spoke of them openly in front of me, all the while taking every precaution to shield from my eyes the carbon copies of his two handwritten sheets. Even as he mocked me, he was dying for me to read this first example of his writing. Then one of the members of his cell took me to a corner and showed me the secret bulletin, making me swear not to breathe a word. Several months later, reconciled again, Nessim admitted that he had been responsible for showing me the secret.

My isolation grew. If I gave in, I could put an end to the torture I was forced to undergo because of my curiosity. But I would be losing face — and to what an extent! I decided to break the bars of silence and make myself heard. Our friendship had slipped imperceptibly down the road of rivalry and now I would have to take up the challenge and prove to Nessim that my gifts for democratic leadership and polemics were as great as his.

My first *engagé* writing was a number of handwritten tracts openly distributed to anyone who asked for them. The title set the tone: it was a denunciation of the secret society. Although I mentioned no names, my real concern was obvious — I wanted to settle my account with Nessim and express the pain I felt at our broken friendship. I denounced the use of weapons and launched an appeal for the union of all Iraqis.

I became involuntarily the spokesman for all those who felt repugnance at crossing swords with the Muslims and who had no taste for preparing for combat. They placed their hope in a return to confidence and understanding.

Iraqi nationalism was coming out of the shadows in which Rashid Ali and his disciples had sunk it, renewed, rejuvenated, unrecognizable. For some Jews it even became the springboard for a new appeal for unity. Let us mend broken friendships, open our hearts, and we will find that we are alike in our desires and aspirations.

Most of our friends were indifferent to the acerbic exchanges Nessim and I indulged in during recreation periods. I could only admit the weakness of my position. I constantly invoked the faces of our numerous Muslim friends and companions. But they remained in the shadows, buried in an immutable silence. Invisible characters, abstractions, the recruits who marched behind Nessim vanished like ghosts.

At the start of the school year, we had little homework and it did not absorb all our time. We spent our spare time in polemics which became as bitter as they were monotonous. They came to a brutal end. The whole school was in a flurry when one of the final-year students disappeared. His unexpected departure was distressing to his family and dozens of students. For the man who had taken flight was none other than the founder and high chief of the secret society. He had taken a small fortune with him. For weeks his teams had sacrificed candy and treats to acquire revolvers. But no weapons were seen in anyone's pockets. The leader took refuge in propitious clandestinity. Even if everyone knew him and discreetly paid him the honour due to his rank, no one had the right to reveal a secret which had ceased to be one.

A week later the leader appeared in the schoolyard. His authority restored calm and silenced doubts. He claimed he had gone to negotiate with mysterious allies. Clandestinity was a convenient protection. He could not be asked for accounts. It was simply known that he must have spent the money collected for buying arms when he was on this important mission. The subscriptions had to be started again, and sweets and treats had to be sacrificed indefinitely.

Nessim realized that he had been the victim of a sad joke and decided to leave the society which, in any case, was crumbling and soon would vanish. If it had been only his pocket money, he would have been easily consoled, but he had invested too many dreams, too much passion, to be able to turn the page. He had to make his feelings public, and the opportunity soon arose.

Every Thursday morning there was a ceremony to mark the start of lessons. We stood in rows but instead of going directly to our classes as we did on other days, we remained where we were to salute the flag. During the first few weeks of school, it had been inconvenient to prolong this collective declaration of our love for a homeland which caused us so much pain. We hastily sang three or four patriotic songs printed on the program of every school in the country; the flag was raised and we went off to our classrooms two at a time.

One Thursday the teacher responsible for the ceremony decided to include the reading of a poem written by a senior student in honour of the king. A harmless tribute, because the monarch was younger than us and his youth relieved him of all responsibility for the crimes committed a few months earlier by his people. The lines had the proper number of feet and — supreme triumph — they rhymed. Obviously proud of his protégé, the teacher presented him to us as an example. We brought down the house. There was a live poet among us and the honour reflected on the whole school. No one would have guessed what this event would lead to. The wall of silence was crumbling and all around us poetic talents were springing up. Each class had its bard who competed with his fellows in patriotic declamations. We memorized so many Islamic and pre-Islamic poems that sang the virtues of various tribes, or praised monarchs or military leaders, that we inevitably followed in the footsteps of our prestigious predecessors.

Nessim realized the importance of this memorable ceremony. Three weeks later he climbed up on the little table used as a platform for those serving their apprenticeship as haranguers of crowds. A mark of distinction: he was the only poet in school who still wore short pants. I was filled with emotion as soon as he declaimed the title of the poem: a hymn to the flag. Nessim was returning to the fold. He was rallying behind the standard that was raised every day by our murderers. What did it matter? We were on the same side again. I had won and I rushed over to tell him how much I admired him before the others got to him. In fact, I wanted to tell him how happy I was to see our friendship triumph over a crisis which was nothing but a misunderstanding. And to seal the rebirth of our friendship, I composed that very evening some lines dedicated to the two rivers that watered the soil of our beloved country.

Soon we felt the prose writers quickening their pace behind us, demanding their share of public honours. I waited impatiently that Thursday morning for the end of the peroration by one of these prose writers who was clumsily recounting the details of the car accident which had claimed the life of King Ghazi.

Our school did not have a monopoly on talent. Each Jewish school had its cluster of poets and prose writers. To stimulate budding writers, two contests were launched simultaneously. One was reserved for the students of the Alliance and the other was open to all the Jewish schools in town.

For months the school was gripped in a fever of writing. Of course only a small minority took part. But we felt behind us suspended hopes, support. Our victories would be those of our class or, more modestly, of a group of friends. Nessim and I were promoted by our friends to the role of standard-bearer for the class. It was an honour which we only half desired. In fact, it confirmed our isolation from the others. We were the literary ones and we willingly conceded a superiority we did not want, because it was considered trivial. What counted was science and mathematics, whose usefulness we could not question, and our inferiority in that area was obvious.

Neither patriotic songs nor literary contests could quench our all-consuming thirst. We decided to put out a weekly newspaper. The school would take care of typing the short stories, poems and criticism.

Nessim had the honours in the first issue. He could not contain his joy. Next day the teacher asked him to read his Arabic composition before the class. He made a mistake in conjugating a verb, a terrible mistake for a writer. He was not pleased to be corrected by the teacher. Anger born of thwarted arrogance turned his face purple. To the audience, to whom he accorded no right but that of admiration, he pointed out, "That mistake will not appear in the printed text."

We claimed a lofty indifference to the results of the contest. We won third and fourth prizes. Our stories would be included in the book that would publish the works of all the winners. Guessing what would most impress us, the teacher responsible for correcting the proofs told us that our names would appear in three different places. When the great day arrived and we finally held in our hands the living proof of our new identity, we were embarrassed at our joy. We kept an eye on each other, ashamed of our excitement. To divert my attention from his trembling hands, Nessim, as usual, turned to joking.

"Your name takes up more room in print than mine does."

With the book under my arm, the streets seemed different. I possessed a secret and I was fully aware of its power. My name was in print, in thick black letters. I felt I was seeing the people in the street for the first time! The woman whose veil only half-covered her rags, the porter barely older than I stalking customers and, behind the donkeys, the road sweepers. They were poor, illiterate. They would not know how to decipher the name of a writer on a page. In a low voice, I told them of my resolution and my promise: "You are living in misery! Look at me: I'm going to change things for you!"

For now I had a power, the power of my signature. Today an anthology, tomorrow the newspapers. I would defend the poor and the oppressed. These men and women were walking with ignorance written on their faces. Now they had a new spokesman.

Before I went to sleep, I put the book under my pillow and during a restless night I kept assuring myself that the precious object was still there.

When the result of the contest in all the schools was made public, Nessim's and my enthusiasm was truly launched. Without discussing it, we both resolved to reach a real audience. Nessim wrote poems for each of the papers and I bombarded the weekly and monthly magazines with stories. Our elders did not even take the trouble to send us rejection notices. Still prolific, we regularly mailed off our manuscripts. Finally, the oppressive silence was broken. One day my mother handed me a white envelope. Three short lines. The editor-in-chief of an avant-garde literary magazine had read my story and wanted to meet me. I could go to his office any afternoon. I was so excited that I jumped up and down. I wanted to tell my mother. Useless. She would not appreciate the implications. I was dying to shout: the man who wrote this letter is the greatest writer in our country!

I was already dreaming of the visit. I mentioned to my mother that I was old enough now to wear long trousers.

"Your brother wore short pants until he was sixteen. And you know how much a suit costs."

I still had two years to wait before I would be entitled to dress like a man.

When my mother asked me where the letter had come from, I told her, "Oh, it's nothing."

"What do you mean?"

"Oh, it isn't important."

The next day after school I went to the offices of the magazine. I wandered cautiously through the unfamiliar streets, in the heart of the Muslim section. The fear of the Jew moving through enemy territory was mixed with the emotion I felt at the coming confrontation with the great writer.

I found myself in the red-light district. Impelled by a powerful curiosity, I automatically slowed down. In this place of perdition my nascent virility made me forget my fear. These women had all the attractions I had dreamed about. I had only to cross the street. They were no longer part of the world of dream and imagination. Would I dare to cross the threshold? Two policemen standing at the door searched every visitor. Anyone with a dagger or a revolver who had come to wash his stained honour had to be kept aside. Until they slit the throat of the offending woman, whether sister, daughter or cousin, they would be covered with disgrace. So pressing was my desire to be initiated into manhood before seeing the editor-in-chief that I hardly trusted myself to cross the guarded doorway alone. But my short pants gave me a good argument to get out of the situation. I walked faster, seized by the fear that someone would surprise me in my lust.

The magazine office and the editor's house were in the same building. I knocked at the door. A little girl opened it. I uttered the name of the master. The child could not take her eyes off me. Without moving she shouted, "Baba, a boy wants to see you."

"Tell him to come up."

A dimly lit staircase took me to that lair of the intelligentsia, the editorial offices of a magazine. Here important decisions were made, talents discovered, the future of Iraqi literature planned, the fate of writers sealed. The only furniture was a small desk painted dark red, two chairs and, stacked on a wooden shelf, a few books and copies of the magazine.

Tall and robust, the editor looked like a giant, which only increased my emotion.

I had forgotten he was a teacher. His students must have been boys my own age, and he was correcting exercises. He had small eyes in a florid face.

"Yes, son?" he said, barely raising his head.

My heart beat harder and harder. For him I was just a child. I should never have come in short pants. He wouldn't take me seriously. I whispered my name. This time the writer looked up resolutely. He discovered that it was broad daylight.

"Yes, where is he?" he said, looking at me.

I repeated my name and placed my fingertips against my chest. "It's me."

He burst out laughing.

"I was positive it was your older brother."

His voice changed. He pointed to one of the chairs. I sat on the edge, straight as a stick.

"Congratulations, *ustadh*."

Ustadh! Was he making fun of me, calling me master? He assured me of his support. I was among "the great hopes of Iraqi literature." Was he apologizing for the patronizing tone he had used earlier? And did his excessive politeness not prove he did not take me seriously? Yet he made no allusion to my short pants and did not even seem to notice them.

I soon became my voluble self and told him how much I admired his work.

"From now on, think of your own work as well," he said solemnly.

When my mother saw me, she let out a cry of relief: I had come back safe and sound. My father had just told her that when he went to look for me at school, they said I had left at the usual time and no one knew where I was.

My father threatened to beat me for upsetting the whole family. Didn't I know that anything could happen to a boy my age wandering outside the protection of his own district! My mother told me she was angry yet she could not hide her joy at seeing me, still smiling over my triumph. Wait till they learned about the status the greatest writer in the land had just accorded me.

"Explain yourself," my brother said calmly.

When my explanation had been given, I waited for shouts of admiration.

"That's all very well," my brother replied, "but you mustn't neglect your studies."

My mother, paying little attention to the details, was content to say, "You should have let us know."

FOUR OR FIVE GREAT EVENTS stood out in our school year: the performance at the cinema offered at a reduced price by the school, the bicycle trip to a model farm and, most of all, the annual visit to Babylon.

Two or three cars in the train were reserved for our trip to Babylon. As we set out, we could already taste adventure. We unwrapped fruit, hard-boiled eggs, omelettes and chicken legs. The more modern opened cans of sardines. Each of us had enough for four or five meals and when we were no longer hungry we tried to stimulate our gluttony through variety. We would trade a pear for a peach, an orange for a banana. We did not stop singing and shouting.

Every time the train stopped, we had our pictures taken with the natives, fixing for posterity our meeting with these distant people.

When we arrived in Babylon, we visited the ruins, strolling across the remains of the hanging gardens, admiring canals and streets that were more highly perfected than the contemporary villages along the way. In the midst of the ruins, the decapitated lion still had all its majesty. Some of us were allowed to climb up the plinth and straddle the grey statue.

An arid city, without vegetation, surrounded on all sides by the desert. We looked eagerly for a dark corner where we could continue to nibble at our interminable snack.

Our history teacher tried hard to impress us with the antiquity of Babylon. Twenty-five centuries! He struggled to awaken our curiosity about his ancestors. But nothing connected us to them until the day when the English teacher was our guide. Then Babylon burst from the shadows, the hanging gardens were resplendent in the sun, the streets swarming with voices that sounded like our own. We could have heard his words in our sleep, from beyond the grave. That day our English teacher showed us the true history of the city.

"Only the Jews can feel the upheaval of a living past under these piles of stones," he told us. "Nothing ties the Arabs to Babylon. When they conquered it, we were already there. We are the true natives. We came here as captives, the slaves of Nebuchadnezzar. But we triumphed over defeat. On this ground we wrote the Talmud. The descendants of captives, the sons of slaves were great scholars, great philosophers. Are we worthy of our ancestors?" he exclaimed. "We should be ashamed of our laziness."

And how did he end his speech? By exhorting us to work

hard, to study English, the key that would open the doors of the world to us.

When we came back that day, I did not feel like singing or eating. Huddled among the other sleepy travellers, I could not sleep. Eyes closed, I saw myself barefoot, burned by the sand, a burden on my back, beside my captive brothers, crossing the desert, the rivers and the plains. Our backs were straight and instead of lowering our heads, we closed our eyes to the scene of our humiliation. We were preparing to give the world the Talmud, that treasure of infinite wisdom.

TWELVE

I HAD GREAT ADMIRATION for our French teacher. He came from Thessalonika and he had studied at the Ecole Normale Orientale in Paris before the war. He spoke to us of La Fontaine, of spring in Paris, the flowers, the trees turning green. I looked forward to the day when he would assign a French composition. Then he would discover the writer in the class. When the day arrived, disdaining the subject he had written on the blackboard, I wrote out the first four pages of a short story which, because of a lack of time, unfortunately remained unfinished. But he knew all the secrets of the craft; he would understand. On the day he was to return our work, I walked around the schoolyard, the only party to the great secret. I spoke loudly to my classmates and kept even Nessim ignorant.

I walked calmly into the classroom, not even glancing at the infants around me.

The teacher read three or four compositions of depressing banality.

"I've kept the worst composition for last," he said, and stared at me.

"Not only did you not deal with the subject but you've given me an unbelievable piece of gibberish."

"But I'm a writer!" I said. "I won a prize in the story contest. I've been published in an Arabic literary magazine."

He did not laugh at me, nor did he show any surprise. He asked me to translate the prize-winning story into French so he could read it. I did so that evening. He read it the next day, during recreation period, and returned it to me immediately.

"It isn't beautiful."

But I was proud of the "ideas" the story contained.

"Everybody has ideas. Books are full of them."

He advised me to read the great French writers. I told him the ones I had read in translation: Michel Zévako, Alphonse Carr, Victor Hugo. He was in charge of the school's French library and he would supervise my reading. That day he handed me a novel by the Comtesse de Ségur. I spent the whole evening and part of the night looking for the beauty in it but it remained cloaked in the deepest mystery. The work showed me only its puerility. Were all Europeans so childish? The next day I vigorously expressed my disappointment to the teacher.

"I gave you that book for the language. You have to get used to reading in French before you tackle more serious writers."

For several months, dictionary in hand, I read only French authors. French children did not seem to be ashamed of their age as much as we were. I let myself be guided blindly by the teacher as far as the choice of books was concerned. Daudet was followed by Anatole France. I didn't even have the pleasure of discovery.

"Now you can choose the books you want to read yourself," he announced after several months.

From then on my appetite was given free rein. A new world was bursting open before me. Distant Europe was assuming a shape. In novels, women were real. Men talked to them, watched them walking in broad daylight, openly expressed their wishes.

One day on a shelf I discovered the whole series *Cahiers de la Quinzaine*. My teacher told me that the Alliance paid for all its schools to subscribe in order to help Péguy survive. The yellowed pages broke when I folded them. And that was how I discovered Jean Christophe, who had been published in this series. I identified with this French adolescent who had heard the call to depart and answered it. I dreamed of Sabine and of all the women he had known. I copied out pages so that I could reread them after the book was returned.

Nessim looked sulky and sneered at my new reading matter. He considered it a retreat into childhood to read, even in French, books that did not belong to our times. His great discovery was the Lebanese poet Kahlil Gibran. He already knew his poems by heart. Our conversations were often reduced to an exchange of quotations. We were living in two worlds that we revealed to one another with fervour and proprietary jealousy. We had been quick to tell each other of our discoveries and soon we began to admire the same things. I was disappointed when I talked with my French teacher about Gibran and he admitted, quite unembarrassed, that he had never heard of him. Was it possible for a cultivated European not to know the name of such a great writer?

For us, Romain Rolland and Gibran, so far apart, so different, expressed the same revolt, muffled by a diffuse spirituality, a vague mysticism. Their cries and their appeals were transformed into a subtle evasion that allowed us too to escape from a world that struck us as unreal and abstract, because it was so narrow. We did not take refuge in dreams but transplanted ourselves outside our stifling existence into the enchanted mountains and villages of Lebanon, the forests of Europe and the women of the West. They walked before us, far more real than the veiled shadows who populated the streets of our city.

We consumed quantities of newspapers and magazines. Contributing to several monthly publications, we felt responsible for the entire Iraqi press. There was one large obstacle left for us to clear: the means to buy them. For even when we shared the expenses, we were far out in our calculations.

We didn't dream of asking our parents for money. Our school expenses and clothes already caused serious problems. I didn't even dare to tell my mother about my concerns. But one day when I saw my sister holding a red lipstick, I was overcome with rage. It was unreasonable to squander money on trifles when we needed it so desperately. My mother simply told me it was none of my business. And my sister, who these last few weeks had often heard me singing the praises of western women, told me that lipstick must not be completely useless since the women I admired so much certainly made use of it.

It was Nessim who found a solution to our problems. If we needed money, we would have to earn it. Starting the next week he would give private lessons.

"I asked the Arabic teacher to give my name when parents ask him to recommend a student to help their children."

The same day I went to speak to our French teacher. He told me he gave private lessons himself and that he was pleased at my desire to do so, since he received more requests than he could handle.

A few days later my teacher already had the name of a student for me. Her parents had asked a woman teacher from the girls' school but she already had too much work. Under the circumstances, my age and short pants were my most important qualities. I would not represent any danger to the virtue of the young girl who was two or three years older than me. She was repeating all her courses and she had not yet managed to receive her primary certificate. She was already engaged and her future husband, a doctor, wanted his wife to be a graduate.

She had a very beautiful face and, a rare privilege in Baghdad, her eyes were limpid blue. Her fair complexion and auburn hair had attracted requests for marriage, especially because her parents were adding a generous dowry to her trousseau.

We sat in a corner of the living room, whose windows looked out on the river. To reassure themselves about my behaviour, the members of the family would always choose this moment to admire the boats and barges crossing the Tigris. If it wasn't the grandmother, it was the young sister and sometimes even the maid. These witnesses embarrassed me and affected my pedagogic abilities, particularly because my pupil admired the river as much as the other members of her family. Often, right in the middle of a laborious explanation, I would notice that instead of listening to me she was conversing, with many winks and gestures, with her sister or the maid.

From time to time, drawn by a cry or shout, she would get up to make sure they weren't dredging out a drowned man. Her generous bosom would then come dangerously close to my face. I dared not look at her like a man. But as soon as I turned my back and started home, I gave my imagination free rein. I even managed to forget the strong odour given off by her armpits, which on particularly hot days made me sick. Her animal splendour erased any memory of her exasperating absent-mindedness and the mediocrity of her intelligence.

One afternoon she was so attracted by a barge being towed by a bargeman that she left her seat and stood right at the window. I was no longer the timid boy I had been during the first lessons. Correcting her dictation, I warned her that she would fail the next examinations. Bewildered, she stared at me and without opening her mouth began to weep silently. Tears poured down her cheeks. I was more embarrassed than disturbed. And I felt contempt for this beautiful girl who instead of reacting to my warning was reprimanding me with her tears. I, who had imagined that women were filled with softness, resplendent with charm, now felt all the femininity of her body vanish. And yet her eyes had not lost their glow and her breasts were still just as round. For the first time, a woman was crying in front of me, because of me; and I was annoyed at her for destroying my dream.

The next day they thanked me for my services, invoking my youth.

THIRTEEN

IN THE FOLLOWING WEEKS I had several other pupils — young boys, usually the class dunces. The father of one of them played poker with an august Muslim who had married a waitress, a Germanic beauty, while he was studying in Berlin. This union had produced the jewel of the family, which still had ties with Bedouin tribes. She had her mother's green eyes and her father's dark complexion, Germanic authority, oriental docility and a vivacity that was hers alone. Her father intended her to travel and to study even if there was no lack of marriage offers. Two ambassador uncles had offered to supervise her education. Before she left she would have to be introduced to foreign languages. My services were required.

She lived near me, in the Al Sadoun neighbourhood. The houses there were surrounded by vast lawns, bordered with trees. To get to her house, I went along a street where the neighbourhood prostitutes lived.

This Muslim girl's parents feared me less than the parents of my Jewish pupil. Her mother received me with courtesy and then left us alone. Though the girl wore the veil, the *abaya*, to go to school, she left her face uncovered and offered its secrets to every passerby.

I went to her house twice a month. At first I kept my eyes on my books, not daring to look at her. Then, growing braver, I would sneak glances at her half-naked arms and at her breasts.

She was concentrating on her French speller, making rapid progress and seeming completely indifferent to me. When she congratulated me for the article I had published in a newspaper, I felt the dam was going to burst. I confided in her about my plans for the future. Would she like to read my stories? Of course, but for the moment she wanted to make use of my literary talent in another way. She had an Arabic composition to write. She had no ideas. Could I make some suggestions? Give her some ideas? Of course, but would it not be better if I wrote the composition myself? She agreed. That evening I wrote feverishly, dreaming of the admiring looks that would be my reward.

When I walked down the prostitutes' street on my way to her house the next day, I was no longer sighing with desire but with pity and commiseration. There were few customers late in the afternoon. The women, dressed casually but no less seductively, were warming themselves in the sun, on their balconies, brushing their clothes or painting their faces. I stared avidly at them. Usually they laughed at my short pants and treated me to an obscenity. Today, strong in my secret, I walked calmly, glancing at them indifferently. I had something better. Perhaps my pupil harboured a secret passion for me.

When I handed her the finished work, she counted the pages and thanked me profusely. She apologized for having to cut out several passages, because her teacher would wonder whether she had filled all these pages herself.

We took up the French speller. Our relationship had not undergone the slightest change. Did I have a place in her thoughts?

Her confident eyes and spontaneous smile were unexpectedly beautiful. I was overflowing with projects and dreams. She listened to me, encouraged me to go on. Would I ever dare to make the leap into the unknown, tell her that I loved her, that I could love her? In the innocence of our youth we could still speak freely to one another. I was the boy she could follow with a gesture, a glance. I would never threaten her femininity because I could never be a man for her. A Muslim, member of a distinguished family, she would go to Europe or America, following her diplomat uncles. Then she would marry the son of a minister or a young officer. She was a prisoner, while I was totally free. I had the freedom of the male, and that of the Jew as well. I would not become a diplomat or an officer, nor was there anything else in store for me. Did she envy me? No, because she knew what efforts and ordeals I would have to undergo.

Our conversations grew longer, but no one was concerned. From time to time the maid would bring us lemonade or water. She was the only person who interrupted our tête-à-tête.

I accepted the gifts of the moment and did not want to destroy, through a rash hope of love, the presence that was so generously offered to me.

"You're coming home late," my mother said one day when my lesson had gone on for more than two hours.

"You know where I was. I wasn't having fun, I was working."

"Your lessons last a lot longer than an hour."

"So?"

Embarrassed at having broached such a delicate subject, and probably ashamed of her suspicions, she took great pains to remind me that my pupil was a girl and I was a man.

I was flattered by her concern, but I also found it strange that we were left alone, that no one ever took it upon themselves to supervise us. Was there really no danger to be expected from me?

"Who can say what might happen when you leave a young girl alone with a man?" my mother said. "Perhaps her mother doesn't know the difference between Baghdad and Europe. And most of all, you mustn't forget that you're a Jew and she's a Muslim. These things always come to a bad end and a Jew isn't forgiven."

"What things?"

She didn't really know. For such things never happened in our city. If a Muslim ran away with a Jewish girl in the poorest levels of society, the girl would generally end up in a brothel. Otherwise we would have been waging a perpetual religious war.

Rarely had I seen my mother so upset. She was not reproaching me for my behaviour; she was afraid. It would take just a few mischief-makers to raise doubts about the purity of my intentions, to bring down serious threats. A Muslim's stained honour is always avenged. But these fears seemed so out of proportion to the sad reality of our innocent conversation.

"You're still young and you don't know about women. They get carried away very easily. They lack judgement."

I reassured my mother. I had decided, I told her, never to prolong the lesson again.

I began to be afraid, not for the honour of the girl who needed no one to defend her, but for myself. Love could be born, in spite of prohibitions, obstacles and threats. There was a basis for my mother's concerns. I was going to fall in love, already had in fact, but I forbade myself any declaration that would have meant submitting to an impossible fate.

The whole family was convinced that I was walking on the edge of a precipice. They alluded only indirectly to the dangers. Whenever I was nearby, my sister and grandmother chose to pick up the story of the misfortune of a classmate of my sister's.

There was a moral to the story, and it was intended for me.

Sabiha was the victim of her innocence and of men. At six-teen she was beautiful and healthy, plump, always smiling. Fate was against her family. While her mother went to the bedside of a sick brother every afternoon, her father went to a *mikhana*, a bar, as soon as he had finished work, and did not come home until late at night, dead drunk. When Sabiha came home from school, she was always alone in the house, her two young brothers spending the afternoon playing in the courtyard.

The family lived in a mixed neighbourhood, Jews and Christians living together as good neighbours. Friendships were formed, but they were always broken when the children grew up and there was a risk that they would continue to associate with one another.

Sabiha spent her afternoons at the window. She watched the people going in and out of the three shops across the street, which were occupied by a tailor, a carpenter and a bookseller. She was particularly attracted by the young male students who came to the lending bookstore to trade romantic novels. She would have liked to subscribe to the bookstore too, but she dared not mention it to her mother. Did the school not have a library where books could be borrowed free? Besides, would she have had the audacity to go and ask for a romantic novel in front of so many boys?

A cousin of the owner noticed her several times, standing behind the bars of her window. He became the bookstore's most assiduous customer. He would stare at Sabiha and she would not look away as she should have done. Growing bolder, he gave her a faint smile, without taking his eyes off her. Instead of slam-ming the shutters in his face, Sabiha did not move. She did not even look away. Every day the boy's boldness grew more explicit.

His smile was not hesitant as it had been at the beginning. He made faces and Sabiha could not help laughing. This little game went on for several weeks. One morning when Sabiha was on her way to school, she discovered the boy waiting for her at the corner of the street. She walked past him and neither one was so foolish as to make the slightest smile or gesture. They realized that the whole neighbourhood would know of their secret liaison. As she passed the boy, he bent down without looking at her and picked up a piece of yellow paper which he slipped into her hand, telling her out loud that she had dropped it. She was quick to understand the subterfuge, thanked him and was completely happy with their victorious complicity. In school, Sabiha was trembling with emotion, surprise and joy. Her adventure was bolder than any film or novel.

Having been afraid to unfold the yellow paper on the street, she now hid it under her textbook and began to read the message.

Sabiha was too absorbed to hear the teacher call on her. The woman stood in front of her and demanded that Sabiha give her the note. Trying awkwardly to conceal the paper, Sabiha held out another sheet. But the teacher was intractable. It was the yellow paper that she wanted. For months the yellow paper was the subject of every conversation in and out of school.

Although the teacher, a European from Thessalonika, had only a rough knowledge of Arabic, the highly incriminating nature of the missive could not escape her. She held the weapon in her hand.

"This is a love letter," she kept repeating, "a love letter."

The news spread by word of mouth and soon it was known to the whole family circle: "Sabiha was caught reading a love letter in school." They might have thought they were at the movies!

No one breathed a word about the boy. A heavy silence fell as soon as anyone alluded to his existence. He was a Christian. There was no question of a hasty marriage. He could not even be reproached for his dishonour. He was only playing his role as a man: to pervert a young girl whose naïveté or impure thoughts made her an easy prey. On this side, the matter was closed. Guilty of weakness in the face of degrading advances, Sabiha now had to pay.

In our family the debate resumed every day. My grandmother, mother and sister weighed the pros and cons. Who should be accused? The father who had neglected his responsibilities, the mother who lacked vigilance, or Sabiha, the pitiful victim? Should one blame her silliness or rejoice at the punishment she so richly deserved? My mother blamed the teacher.

"Isn't she a woman herself? Doesn't she expect to have a daughter some day? She should have realized that a public denunciation was the same as a sentence with no right of appeal. She should have kept the letter and warned the family immediately. And people say that Europeans have good judgement, that they're educated. She must have seen love letters in Paris."

Sabiha's family adopted the attitude that was required in the circumstances. They concealed their shame under a mantle of modesty. Rejecting Sabiha, refusing her any protection, would have led her inevitably along the road to perdition. And a prostitute would stain the family's name forever. Even distant cousins would have found fewer takers on the marriage market. In this hour of adversity, all the relatives joined ranks to save the spoils, to find her a husband, no matter who.

Her mother had entertained great hopes in the past: her daughter was beautiful, healthy, the product of a family whose past was innocent of any blemish. She could easily have found a young, rich husband from an excellent family who would have taken her with just her clothes as a dowry. Now it was only a dream. Aunts, uncles, cousins of both sexes met to sift through all the possibilities before sounding out the candidates. Finally, an intermediary presented the rare bird: a rich man who would accept Sabiha with just her clothing — that is, with no dowry. The family had nothing else to offer. No property to mortgage, no jewels to sell. The applicant did not present only good qualities. No one wanted to examine his past troubles or know the exact nature of the disease that had kept him apart from people for several years. Naturally he did not come from a family of which one could be proud. In spite of all the evidence, the intermediary declared with quiet conviction that the family did not harbour any fallen woman or thief or even a bankruptcy. None of its members had died of tuberculosis or any other shameful disease. And troublemakers who spread false rumours about a cousin of the boy who was in an insane asylum should not be believed. This family had no reason to envy the most honourable families in the city. The applicant's great-grandfather had even been a rabbi.

There was only one problem: the candidate was almost sixty, even though the *dellal* said that he was just past forty. "It would be wrong to make that an obstacle to a happy marriage," he said. "A mature, thoughtful man knows how to treat a woman." Particularly because the future husband was in full possession of all his faculties. Neither deaf nor weak-sighted, he did not even wear glasses. "He's in better shape than most boys ten or even twenty years younger," he added. "And besides, our lives are in God's hands. Death doesn't ask our age when it comes knocking at the door."

Yes, the *dellal* knew very well that some people claimed his candidate was not handsome. "Since when is beauty a masculine quality?" he exclaimed. "Besides, people's looks are a matter of taste. Isn't it lucky to find a man nowadays who will accept a woman with no trousseau, clothe her, buy her a big house, furnish it for her, hire servants? Your daughter will be treated like a princess, a queen," he concluded.

There was no more reason to hesitate. Under normal circumstances, it would have been superfluous to ask Sabiha's opinion. Now that she had been compromised, it would be completely out of the question.

When the engagement was announced three weeks after the discovery of the letter, conversation was revived. Sabiha had not set foot inside the school since the bleak event. Now she had more pressing reasons for ending her studies. Two months later she was living in her own house with her servants, her new furniture and her silver. She was even entitled to a sumptuous wedding which, contrary to custom, was paid for by the husband.

FOURTEEN

NOT ALL YOUNG GIRLS had Sabiha's luck and it was not always possible to recover one's virtue. Another girl, Saida, had taken the road to perdition to the very end. I often used to see her when I came home from school, roaming through the neighbourhood, looking at her former classmates as they strolled by, books under their arms.

Outrageously made up, dressed in bright colours, there was no doubt about the kind of life she was leading. In our neighbourhood of schools and synagogues, houses of ill fame were rare and prostitutes did not usually venture out without concealing their shame beneath the veil. Saida's appearance inevitably set off a commotion. The adolescent boys, whose virility was just awakening, led off. They would hound the girl who dared to walk about in broad daylight with her face uncovered. They would shout in chorus: Prostitute, prostitute.

Sometimes they would run behind her, throwing stones. Saida would give back as good as she got. She would insult them, shout vulgar words at them. That was when her grandmother would intervene. She was always there, accompanying the child in her daily pilgrimage down the street of her school. She begged her to be calm, to ignore the young hoodlums and walk faster.

"You know that they're wicked and bad-mannered," the grandmother would say. And turning to the boys, she would shout, "Aren't you ashamed? Don't you fear God?"

Like most of her friends, my sister would lower her eyes and walk past the girl. She was afraid of catching the eye of her former friend. Who knows, she might be contaminated. Saida's crime was so horrible that she hoped it would never turn up even in her worst nightmares. It was a plague which, at the slightest inattention, could touch you and destroy you.

Was Saida as beautiful as she seemed to my avid eyes? In the days when they used to leave school with their arms around one another's waist, I used to find her as seductive as my sister.

My grandmother overwhelmed Saida. She was triumphant. Her predictions had been confirmed. Had she not warned my sister time and again about that insolent girl whom no one supervised? She had been three years old when her mother died. Her father, a poor humble man, worked relentlessly to bring her up and send her to school. Her grandmother gave in to all her whims.

"That girl will turn out badly," my grandmother predicted as soon as she noticed her with my sister.

Then Saida "fell," that is, she crossed the line separating future wives and mothers from the residents of brothels. No one knew exactly how it happened or who was responsible for her fall. The name of a Jewish writer was mentioned. He was one of the founders, most of them Jewish, of the only weekly literary publication in Baghdad, the platform for an incipient élite which was preparing for the coming of an autonomous literature. Young lawyers, officials, students, their enthusiasm was all the more powerful because it had been repressed. I read avidly their poems, translations and stories. There was nothing Jewish about what they were doing: they were writers, Iraqis.

Despite her youth, Saida was a diligent reader of the paper. She dreamed of love and adventures like the ones that had caused the suffering of Kais and Laila, Paul and Virginie and all the other fictional heroes.

Inspired by these impassioned lives, she apparently committed the fateful act. Some people claimed she had expressed her admiration for one of the editors of the paper in a passionate letter. Others said she had asked the editor for an appointment to submit a story she hoped to publish.

Whatever happened, the young writer took advantage of her to appease his own base instincts. My brother, who knew the boy well, assured us he could not have committed such an ignominious act. On the contrary, he was apparently madly in love with Saida and had the firm intention of marrying her. While he waited, he had taken her to a *maison de passe*, the only place where a boy and girl could be alone without any risk. Unfortunately the landlord, having noticed Saida's beauty, did the rest.

One day when my sister was bemoaning the fate of her old friend, my brother put his books aside and broke his habitual silence.

"Is what happened to Saida any worse than what happened to Jamil's wife?"

The night before, we had gone to visit our paternal grandmother, who had become a friend of her Muslim neighbours. Jamil, an officer around thirty years old, lived with his father, an official in the Ministry of Education. His young wife was called Amina. My grandmother, mother and sister had spent part of the afternoon with her. The year before, when there was not yet a shadow of a moustache on my upper lip, I was still able to enter the fragile and vulnerable universe of women. I had been at Amina's honeymoon. She had submitted to my questioning with good grace and a frankness that attested to her naïveté. Scarcely more than an adolescent herself, she was astonished at the incomprehensible events that were occurring in her life. She was neither happy nor sad, neither accepting nor in revolt. With complete neutrality, she experienced her initiation into the secular laws she had never thought of disobeying. She was convinced that the tasks imposed on her were the lot of all women.

Early in the afternoon she would prepare two basins of water, one for her husband, the other for her father-in-law. They liked to bathe their feet when they came home from the office, in hot water in winter, cold in summer. They never ate their meals at the same time, as the father used to take his siesta before coming to the table. Amina ate in the kitchen before the men came home so that she could devote herself completely to them while they ate. She fanned them and chased away the flies which buzzed around their plates. Even in her husband's presence she wore the *aba,* which covered her entire body. She did not go so far as to veil her face in his presence, as she would not have been able to perform her tasks so diligently.

Calling her husband or her father-in-law by name would have shown a lack of respect. The father was Abou Jamil, a title which had been bestowed on him by his friends and acquaintances. But her husband? How would she address him? If they had had a son, her husband would have been entitled to the same treatment as her father-in-law; he would have been given the title "father of," Abou. As she was not crafty enough to discover a subterfuge, she chose never to address him directly. And she hoped with all her might for a son who would put an end to her embarrassment.

As bad luck would have it, this event was long in coming. And so her husband did not have the right to a name. Her father-in-law was growing impatient. Six months had passed since his son's marriage and Amina had given no sign of fertility. His decision was made. He communicated it to his son.

"I give your wife another six months. If she doesn't give you a child within a year, it's because she is sterile. Then you will have to take a second wife."

The six months passed and Amina was still just as recalcitrant at accomplishing her noble woman's duty. Abou Jamil set to work. Progressive, with modern ideas, he decided not to look among the cousins and immediate family for his son's new mate. He decided to conduct his search on neutral ground so as not to provoke the anger of fathers who might have offered their daughters' hands. He would make his choice in Lebanon, especially since a trip to the mountains would spare him the dog days in Baghdad.

There, he left it to the shrewdness of several intermediaries and returned a few weeks later armed with a collection of photographs.

Late into the evening the two men argued. If it had been enough to measure the beauty of each woman, the task would have been less arduous. But they also had to examine the candidate's age, her fortune, her health, her family.

Abou Jamil's inquiry was conducted rapidly, too rapidly. And one could not trust the descriptions, always filled with praise, that the intermediaries wrote on the back of each photograph.

During the weeks of bargaining, Amina's existence was unchanged. Every day she prepared the meals and the basins of water, fanned the men and chased away the flies that pestered them. While they held their secret meetings, she took refuge in her kitchen, weeping at her unfortunate fate.

When the choice was made, Abou Jamil went to Lebanon with authority to act for his son; he signed the marriage deed in his son's name and returned with the legitimate wife.

Then fortune smiled on Amina. Life was stirring in her belly. She did not know how to tell her father-in-law the news. She would have been ashamed to speak of it to her husband. She was filled with fear and did not want to disturb the men's plans. It was Abou Jamil himself who noticed the changes in his daughter-in-law's body. He could not contain his joy.

"Divine generosity is infinite. Two reasons to rejoice instead of one. My son will celebrate his second marriage and the birth of his son at the same time."

Amina's joy was not unmixed. She cried constantly. Would she drain the cup of adversity to the dregs? Would her child be a daughter?

The new wife had moved into the house a week before. She paid only slight attention to the other woman's existence, the woman who legitimately shared her husband's bed.

The new wife, Feyrouz, was more demanding than the first. She intended to take over the kitchen; her recipes were better than those in which Jamil and his father delighted. Having thus imposed the superiority of her country, her natural woman's inferiority was reduced. It was hard for Abou Jamil and his son to deny the exquisite flavour of the Lebanese hummus and the delicious taste of *kibbeh*. They gladly conceded to the newcomer the perfection of her culinary talents. Then Feyrouz demanded that the two men eat at the same time, and she ate with the masters. Was she defending some absurd right? Her motives were purely culinary: the dishes should be eaten hot, as their flavour deteriorated when they were reheated. No one ever thought of inviting Amina to share these dinners. She satisfied her hunger on leftovers and declared that she preferred her rival's cooking, relieved that her presence was no longer required in the kitchen.

When Feyrouz was still a candidate, Abou Jamil had specified to her father that she wear the *aba* in the street; but the woman refused to cover her face. Jamil broke out in a cold sweat whenever he imagined his fellow officers satisfying in their imagination the desires which were exacerbated by her beauty. But Abou Jamil serenely imagined the neighbours' cries of admiration at his judicious choice.

Feyrouz had been there only a week and her demands were already increasing. Perfume, jewels, clothing, were only to please her husband, who had neither the strength nor the desire to discourage such a praiseworthy concern. In a month, the life of the whole neighbourhood had been transformed. Conversations now dealt only with the foreign woman who had upset the peaceful suburb.

Amina had become a mere shadow whirling through obscurity. Her weeping irritated the women who came to visit the expectant mother, hoping to meet the new wife. They reproached Amina for her sorrow. A pregnant woman should thank God and be grateful for her good fortune.

"If she goes on whimpering, she'll harm the child," the neighbourhood women warned.

Since the arrival of Feyrouz, Amina's secret dream was to go home to her parents. Was this not the height of ingratitude? my mother asked. Amina's husband had never deprived her of a meal. He gave her lodging and protection. What was she complaining about — a fate that thousands of women would envy?

My brother, to whom Amina had never shown herself with her face uncovered, defended her with passion.

"Amina is a slave. Any other condition, even a prostitute's, is preferable to hers," he maintained.

He was crushingly sarcastic about Feyrouz, saying she must have been a servant in her own country, and had thrown herself at the wealthy descendant of the Bedouins.

My mother refused to pursue the conversation.

"We aren't in Europe or America," she said.

FIFTEEN

SUMMER WAS DRAWING NEAR and despite my mother's pleas my brother took his bed up to the roof. He might be surprised in his sleep by late spring showers but that didn't discourage him. It was stifling in the bedroom.

It would soon be vacation time. The previous summer, the shadow of the *Farhoud* had not yet been erased and the quest for passports filled our days.

The thought that I might spend the entire holiday at home tormented my mother. She was the one who would suffer the consequences of my sloth. Happily, my brother announced the solution.

The Ministry of Supply had just been established. British officers had all the top positions and a whole troop of interpreters and translators had to be hired. The head translator, the one who hired the assistants, was Kamal, a friend of my brother. My chances of becoming a civil servant were excellent. It was Kamal himself who had made the suggestion to my brother.

The civil service salary would put an end to my financial problems. My grandmother, concerned for my well-being, protested. I shouldn't be looking for a job at examination time. What if I missed my year? My mother brushed these fears aside.

Not only would I pass the tests, I would be among the first without even opening a book. Her confidence did not reassure me; it filled me with terror. I was haunted by the fear of failing.

Kamal, the head translator, was a learned man, an indefatigable reader, prolific author of unpublished manuscripts; but there was another side to his personality, with strange habits and excesses. My brother was proud to know him, even admired him, but he did not speak of him without an edge of sarcasm. For hours he took pleasure in reporting his friend's adventures and misadventures, with obvious feeling.

As Kamal lived near us, it was natural for the first official meeting with my future employer to take place at his house.

Kamal was short, with a bristling moustache and tiny, sparkling eyes. His laugh, violent at first, like lightning, remained in suspension between his stomach and his throat before it finally burst out. To underline the object of his hilarity and ensure the attention of his interlocutor, he would prod the latter with his elbow and tap his arm or back.

Kamal had set up his den in the basement of the house. There he felt in full possession of his power, among his books, papers, files and stacks of letters which he kept in their envelopes.

I had not even stepped inside his study when he held out a letter he had just received from London. Leonard Woolf was thanking him for the poem he had written in memory of Virginia. He began to recite the lines he had dedicated to the great novelist.

"Are you going to publish it?" I asked, both politely and admiringly.

"Publish it? Who for? Who cares about my admiration for Virginia Woolf?"

Kamal knew about the literary happenings in London. No newspaper or magazine escaped his consuming thirst. And his love for his contemporaries did not detract from his loyalty to the great masters of the past. He knew by heart long passages from the main plays of Shakespeare.

He carried on an endless dialogue with an ideal companion who kept a respectful silence. If he gave private lessons, it was to confide the secrets of his wisdom. If one were bold enough to express an objection, it would not irritate him. On the contrary, it would allow him to launch into a new soliloquy. His remarks flowed freely, according to the time and the unpredictable turnings of his mind. An allusion to Napoleon would evoke Emil Ludwig's biography, whose method was different from Zweig's, both of them Jews and victims of Nazi persecution; that denial of the great cultural tradition of Germany, a country which had given the world men of the quality of Goethe, whose *Faust* had been translated by several British translators, the most accomplished being … No one could follow him through his endless labyrinths.

In Baghdad the British Council gave the same examinations as those received by students in London. The questions arrived under seal and many of Kamal's students obtained their B.A. in this way, a degree he himself had been unable to obtain. It was not that he failed to appear along with his pupils every year. Invariably he found the questions badly presented. First he exposed ambiguities and denounced contradictions. Once these traps had been set aside, he attacked the question itself, beginning with an introduction, following the method which he patiently inculcated into his own students. And when at last he was ready to reveal his answer, the allotted time was up.

In the little world of his pupils, past and present, Kamal was surrounded by a legend, which his dietary excesses helped to nourish. Kamal, who was thin, never ate for pleasure or because he was hungry. Often, through simple oversight, he would skip a meal or two. If he came home later than usual in the afternoon, he could never remember whether he had eaten lunch or not. As a precaution, his mother always kept a meal for him which she would reheat.

Early in the winter, a restaurant which served only sandwiches opened near our house. Seated at the counter, Kamal waited for players in a game he was perfecting. As soon as he spotted one on the doorstep, he would order all twelve kinds of sandwiches offered by the restaurant. He ate them in the order in which they appeared on the menu on the wall: cheese, chicken, tomato … Once he had bolted down the whole assortment, he would order a second, this time in the reverse order: tomato, chicken, cheese … If he managed to eat all twenty-four sandwiches without stopping, the bettor was obliged to pay the bill. There were few takers, so Kamal raised the stakes. He would eat thirty-six sandwiches, then forty-eight. My brother, who had seen him consume two dozen sandwiches, said there was no evidence that he had gone beyond this performance.

Kamal had two qualities that were much in demand: his knowledge of English and his capacity for work. He was naturally destined for the civil service and it was at the insistence of one of his former pupils that he had finally agreed to apply.

The British occupation forces contained all the vital services of the Iraqi administration. In this way London took its precautions, intending to nip in the bud any movement like that of Rashid Ali. The British officers had practically created and established the Ministry of Supply, and no important decisions escaped their vigilance.

Imports were becoming increasingly restricted and quotas were set on certain products in order to limit their consumption, a measure which only affected the middle classes; the wealthy could buy whatever they wanted on the black market and the poor couldn't buy the products to which they were entitled anyway. One of the first decisions made by the Ministry was to control imports. Only recognized importers could obtain licences whose cost was proportional to their pre-war transactions. Their profits were guaranteed and if the distribution and selling price of the products were not limited or controlled, the profits even increased. In certain cases the profit margin was so great that it was considered a scandal outside the closed circle of recognized importers. And the number of aspiring importers was growing. Influence games were being played behind the backs of the British officers who appeared naïve and innocent despite the eager way in which they worked. When they attempted to penetrate the mysteries of a closed society, they found themselves at the mercy of the people they worked with, interpreters, translators or assistants who worked feverishly to give their Arabic words only the meaning which suited their own interests and could favour those who paid generously for their goodwill.

During our meeting, Kamal talked about what he had been reading recently, the latest pieces he had written, but he made no reference to the kind of work I would have to do. It was understood that I would be hired. It was not my entry into the civil service which preoccupied him.

"I've been telling your brother for a long time that I'd like to give you private lessons. I've read your articles. You must learn about English literature. I'll consider you a disciple and my lessons will be free."

But before I had time to react, he had changed his mind.

"Unfortunately, I can't give you lessons just now. I only keep pupils who have exams to write. I don't want to work night and day. I'm already terribly behind in my own reading."

He pushed me towards the door with one hand and held my arm with the other.

"And the job?" I had to talk about it before I left. "My brother told me about a job …"

"Oh yes, that's right."

He hesitated briefly, then added, "But that's understood, you start tomorrow morning."

THE OFFICES OF THE Ministry of Supply were over Hasso's store, and they looked like an enormous shed where the employees were stacked on top of each other. Only the director-general and the treasurer had privacy. My father had always spoken of his office as a serious place. Now I would learn the truth. The passages separating the staff were always cluttered. Friends who came for coffee ran into businessmen who were checking on their requests for licences. Canvassers and inter-mediaries greeted one another brightly and exchanged news about their children's health.

There were six assistants who helped Kamal in his tasks. We worked at a single table. Barely seated, Kamal would place a pile of requests for import permits in front of me. They had to be translated into English so the British captain, who would ini-tial each permit before it was signed by the Iraqi director, could become familiar with them in his own language.

My first client wanted to import five thousand *yashmaghs*, men's headdresses, from India.

Nervously I asked my neighbour who had been at work for a week, "How do you translate *yashmagh* into English?"

Without looking up, he replied flatly, "*Yashmagh.*"

"I asked you for the English word," I insisted.

"It's the same thing."

An hour later, Kamal came to inspect my work.

"How many requests have you translated?"

"Two."

"Let me see … But you don't have to translate everything. You just have to show what kind of merchandise it is, how much they plan to import, the country of origin and the name of the applicant. It will go much faster."

"Yes, Kamal."

He gave me a look blazing with anger or indignation. I didn't understand. Instead of working out motives and mysteries, I went back to my translation. Now it was going very quickly, and I didn't even need a dictionary. It was easier to ask my colleagues for the English equivalents of the terms that recurred in each request.

At the end of my first day, I was hurrying out of the office when Kamal held me back. He wanted to speak to me alone, away from any prying ears. I was flattered at having so quickly won the confidence of my superior that I was entitled to a private interview, but I was soon singing another tune.

"A civil servant has to watch his manners," Kamal reproached me. "He can't be scatterbrained or ill-mannered."

I understood less and less. Was he talking to me?

"Of course, you're absolutely right."

He became more direct. "Don't you know how to speak to a superior, to a director?"

"I was respectful to the officer. He spoke to me once and I started my sentence with 'Captain.'"

"I'm not talking about the Englishman. I'm talking about me. You called me Kamal in front of everybody."

"Yes." It was his name, after all.

"Don't you know there are certain forms to use when you're speaking to a superior?"

Gradually the light began to dawn. Kamal was my superior, my boss.

"What should I call you?"

"Sayyed Kamal or Kamal Effendi. Be especially careful when other people are around."

On pay day, as I was going to collect my first month's salary, I realised there had been a slight omission. My name was not on the list of employees.

"You aren't eighteen yet," Kamal said.

"No," I replied, ashamed.

"Legally you shouldn't even be here. You have to have reached the age of reason before you can be hired as a civil servant. But don't worry, I'll look after everything. I'll have the Englishman sign the papers himself, without going through all the Iraqi subordinates. He'll judge you on your merit and you won't have to present a birth certificate or diploma."

I finally received my first salary. Twelve dinars, plus six dinars cost-of-living allowance. It weighed heavily in my pocket, and once I was outside I kept checking that my billfold was still there.

I entered our house modestly. I didn't want my joy to be too obvious. And in the voice of someone who is accustomed to the finer things in life, I announced, "I have a box for the whole family at the Rashid cinema."

My father had never set foot inside a movie house and despite the importance of the occasion he didn't intend to change his habits. As for my brother, he was unimpressed by an invitation from his junior. He claimed he had been going to see the same movie with one of his friends.

SIXTEEN

FOR MANY YEARS the cinema had been our joy and our link with the world. We were admitted into the fascinating intimacy of strange people's houses. Men spoke openly of their love to women who sighed and moaned, who laughed with pleasure, welcoming them without fear, their lips hungry. Around these couples who displayed their feelings and desires without constraint, children skipped and jumped, completing the dream picture. My sister caught a glimpse of the shadow of a hope she dared not entertain. For me, the images were a promise.

We could never afford first-class tickets. My mother and sister had got around that obstacle by going to the afternoon show and, protected by their veils, would ask without shame for third-class tickets. Surrounded by young Muslims — porters, labourers, café waiters — and by unemployed adults, we would crane our necks, taking in images reflected by the movements of a screen aimed directly at us.

The women went in a group. Neighbours, friends. Sometimes my mother persuaded my grandmother that Abdul Wahab or Robert Taylor were really very interesting. My presence, my bare face, risked betraying their secret.

Not a week went by that we did not pay our clandestine visit to the cinema. We avoided recent Arab films, the term being used in the broadest sense because six months after they were first shown they continued to attract a large, impatient audience. When we went to the cinema, it was rarely to see the films of Abdul Wahab and Farid al Attrash.

I had never ventured into a movie theatre by myself. As I was a Jew, the young boys of my age, Christians or Muslims, would have attacked me with kicks and slaps.

The darkness of the cinema emboldened the less courageous of our tormentors. Flanked on either side by two or three black shadows, I would walk through the door of the cinema. No male would dare ignore this solid shield. A veiled woman was even more formidable when it was not known whether she was Jewish or Muslim, a cousin or sister of the boss. And if ever these creatures, buried in the mystery of their veils, called for help, dozens of men would surround the attacker, thereby showing their Bedouin chivalry, hoping in their heart to obtain the offended woman's favours.

An honest woman would not call for help. If a young hoodlum lacked respect for her, she would choose to ignore him, walking past him as though he were invisible, a phantom belonging to a world one does not wish to know.

The better I was able to read the Arabic subtitles on films, the more useful I became. I would explain the plot to my grandmother, sometimes to my mother, leaving my sister free to read along and follow her heroes' adventures without being disturbed.

The Egyptian stars spoke in their own dialect and often the meaning of a word or expression would escape us. On the other hand, the difficulties in which the characters found themselves were so clear that words were not important. Sudden twists in the plot were foreseen and the spectators' joy increased when events turned out happily.

In Arabic films, the plot was of secondary importance. Family disputes and lovers' quarrels served as a background and divided up the interludes between songs which made up the basic structure of the film. The cast was never chosen for their acting ability but for their reputation as singers.

I can still remember the first film of Umm Kulthum, the "swallow of the East." Fat, with the first blush of youth already gone, no one could believe that men would tremble with love at the sight of her. But Umm Kulthum had no need of youth or beauty to make them throb with joy. At the beginning of her career, one had to be prepared for pitched battle at the box office in order to watch one of her films. A few months later the crowd would thin out, but the spectators were louder in their enthusiasm. Those who were hearing the songs for the twentieth or thirtieth time could not contain their emotions. They would leave their seats and sing the familiar tunes along with the artist. At the end of each song, wanting to share their joy with the whole audience, they would chant *Allah Allah, Ya Ruhi*.

ON THE EVENING that I took the women of my family to the Rashid cinema, I helped my grandmother sit down and explained the plot to my mother with a patience that surprised her. For years my mother had never missed a chance to remind me of the duties which were incumbent on me. If a quarrel broke out between my sister and me, she would firmly put an end to it. Turning to me, she would give me her most formidable rebuke: "Don't forget that you're a man."

On this night, with my recently acquired authority, I gestured to the candy seller, offered candy to the others and took out my billfold.

At the intermission, my mother said, "Zaki has just bought his mother a coat."

Did she want to destroy my newly won confidence?

"Did he? With what?" I asked, incredulous and mocking.

"With his salary. He's very well paid. Gourjiah keeps singing his praises."

Zaki, the son of my mother's cousin Gourjiah, was two years older than me. He had left school after his primary studies and for two years he had gone from café to café, offering an assortment of merchandise to the men puffing on their *nargilehs* and playing backgammon. He would go hoarse as he praised the high quality and low prices of his razor blades, toothbrushes, shoelaces and other notions. When I went to the café with my father, it was not without shame that I watched him stroll between the chairs. Was I not one of the privileged, I who could peacefully continue my studies?

Despite his lack of training, Zaki's ascent was dazzling. His first job put him in contact with a more select clientele than the habitués of the cafés. He worked in a hotel where, among other duties, he was in charge of greeting the guests. He took their baggage to their rooms and brought them the drinks they ordered. He knew that kindness lavished on important men would always bring returns. Busybodies whispered that Zaki was pushing kindness past the required limits and that he offered the hotel guests services of a very personal nature. A half-dozen young girls counted on his help to meet strangers and local personalities. Of course he had no interest in prostitutes; the women he invited to the guests' tables were of another category.

His sustained contacts with strangers helped Zaki perfect

his English, opening new doors. Had he left the hotel of his own free will, or had the hotel's administration decided he had gone past the bounds?

A store specializing in foreign food products urgently needed English-speaking salesmen, as the presence of the British armed forces had greatly increased its clientele. Zaki was hired, and for three months his house became a sampling centre where friends and neighbours tasted exotic products. His mother, Gourjiah, served sausage, reassuring them of the quality of the meat, declaring that it did not contain a trace of pork. Oranges or apples were no longer eaten at her house. Now they had a completely unknown fruit which was available in cans: strawberries.

The older people tasted the strange products hesitantly, not sure whether they liked them. But the young people, eager to adopt western tastes, were lavish in their praise.

"Zaki should get a director's salary," they exclaimed.

"Of course," his mother would say with satisfaction, "but everything he brings home is free."

But suddenly the manna disappeared, and the same tongues that had delighted in the products now began to whisper. Zaki had been caught red-handed, stealing. The store manager, wanting to spare the young boy from prison, simply showed him the door.

"A boy as intelligent as Zaki causes jealousy," the mother explained.

Happily, Zaki's luck had not run out completely. His sensitive ears picked up the news that the Ministry of Supply was about to open. He appeared before the recruiting officers, and was hired on the spot. As he could barely write English, he was used mainly as an interpreter. He began his new career as duty interpreter and was at the disposal of all the officers. Within two weeks, Zaki had managed to win the confidence of the soldiers.

It was then that the captain appeared on the scene. He was new in the country and was not familiar with the customs or the language. He soon noticed the alert, hard-working boy who did not lounge in the corridors or spend hours drinking tea or lemonade. Zaki put himself at the captain's disposal, not only inside the Ministry but outside as well. He found him a cook and a servant, and in the early days he looked after his shopping and drove him to the furniture merchants.

Warned about the natives' propensity for baksheesh, the captain thanked God for placing such a rare exception in his path. Apparently Zaki mentioned other services he could render, recalling certain acquaintances, occasional tenants of the hotel where he had gone through his first campaign. The captain, who had a dread of tropical diseases, turned a deaf ear. Nevertheless, he was grateful for Zaki's zeal, and a few weeks later he no longer refused to go to certain hotels.

Gourjiah's house had never known such affluence. Distant cousins, friends recommended by half-cousins, came to visit. Zaki became a valuable man, informed about world events, and people came to consult him, ask his opinion on the progress of the war. He made predictions, quoting the Englishman whose authority none could deny. Zaki was the repository of his opinions, interpreter of his forecasts.

I knew that if Zaki's behaviour was condemned, it was only a gesture. Robbing the government was an act of justice, a way of redressing the balance. Few people would hesitate to have a hand in it. And Zaki didn't even go that far. He accepted only gifts and payments that businessmen were happy to offer him.

At the office of the Ministry of Supply, Zaki never missed a chance to point out that we were related. He often went past my office, lingered, besieging me with jokes, making the most ostentatious display of the familial affection he felt for me, introducing me as his very dear cousin. I was his guarantee of good behaviour and the family emblem of respectability.

Of course the businessmen were careful never to speak openly of bribes. And if someone made the slightest allusion to it, whether to clear Zaki of suspicion or to praise or slander those who grew rich on such practices, Zaki would react vehemently. "What do you take me for? People in my family don't take bribes. I wasn't born at Abou Sifain or Souk Hennuni. Do I look like a Muslim?"

The sums he received were destined for the Englishman: he kept nothing for himself.

One day Zaki passed my office. Dazed and white, he saw nothing and no one. I experienced a few moments of anguish. Had someone died in the family?

Kamal's thundering laugh made me jump.

"His Englishman has gone. Flown away, disappeared, vanished."

He could not contain his joy.

We never knew whether the captain had been denounced by a disappointed businessman or an envious official, or whether he had been named to another post.

"Perhaps he's pushing back Rommel's assault," Kamal suggested. "After all, the English are at war and the officers have other jobs to do besides advising Iraqis in their offices and bars."

Zaki remained at his post, reduced to his official powers and salary. His new "Englishman" did not require his services outside the office.

SUMMER WAS ENDING. Soon the holidays would be over. I had been harbouring a project that I didn't dare talk about: to leave school and keep my job. I could continue my education at night.

But one morning I found a form on my desk that I was asked to complete. I was about to be confirmed in my position and my file had to be brought up to date. Simply a matter of routine. Birthplace, age, education, degrees. I acceded without even thinking about it and, like all Kamal's other assistants, I returned the questionnaire to the personnel office. The next day I was summoned to the office. The head of the department asked me to take a seat, bowing his head slightly.

"Are you happy with your work, son?"

"Yes."

"How long have you been working in the Ministry?"

"Three months."

"Who hired you?"

"Sayyed Kamal, with the Captain's consent."

"You state on the form that you're sixteen."

"Yes, I turned sixteen this summer."

"We're happy to have honest boys who are hard-working and intelligent too. But you know the rules. You have to be eighteen to work for the government. With your acquaintances and connections, you can easily find a job in a bank or in business. But we aren't allowed to keep you here."

My face turned purple. I was ashamed of my age and my Jewish "connections."

"Your superiors are completely satisfied with you," he said consolingly. "There are nothing but good reports in your file. Even though your hiring was irregular, we'll give you a reference."

SEVENTEEN

ESSIM AND I were relieved to go back to school. We missed our monthly salaries and the independence it gave us, but we had the compensation of long hours of leisure and our thirst for reading. During the summer, we had seen each other rarely, and the first thing we did when we were back at school for a week was compare notes about our vacations.

Nessim's had been much more fruitful than mine. He had worked in the Censor's office. They had not entrusted him with reading letters written in English or French, or in Arabic. His domain was clearly defined. He was one of the three censors assigned to examining Arabic letters written in Hebrew characters.

Every Jew, no matter how unlettered, began by learning the mysteries of this code. Nessim, who had never felt the need to learn this calligraphy reserved mainly for the old and uneducated, had quickly learned to decipher it after starting to work at the Censor's office. The Muslims often expressed their envy of Jews who had access to this secret writing, called Suki. For us it was a paltry mystery. One had only to know the Hebrew alphabet in order to transcribe our Arabic dialect into this secret language.

These hieroglyphs provided Iraqi businessmen from Java to Manchester with a valuable and formidable weapon because they had the monopoly on it.

Nessim spent days reading handwritten missives in which family news was discussed along with the rates of commissions. Weddings were arranged, inheritances discussed. News was passed on about couples who weren't getting along, and about the health of cousins and mothers-in-law. As an unknown depository of the secrets of the leading families, Nessim felt he had a certain power over them.

Arabic letters, the most numerous, naturally went to the Muslim censors. The Christians and Jews took care of the rest. Not all the Jews were natives. The British army, which supervised the operation of the Censor's bureau, had recruited four or five European Jews in Palestine, each of whom knew about a dozen languages.

Nessim became a friend of a young Palestinian who introduced him to a mysterious individual named Sereni, with whom Nessim began to discuss Judaism and Communism. One day Sereni told him that he was leaving for an unknown destination. As a souvenir, he gave him an unusual volume: the Bible. Nessim did not understand until much later the meaning of the gift, symbol of a growing friendship. Sereni was parachuted by the British army into his native Italy. Arrested by the Germans, he would share the fate of six million European Jews.

Nessim spoke of Sereni with all the enthusiasm of a recent convert. This was how he discovered a personal Judaism, living and Biblical.

Despite Nessim's declarations about our responsibility for building a new and independent Iraq, it was obvious that he only half believed it.

We wrote a great deal — articles, stories, poems. And our studies took up most of our time. We had two examinations to prepare for: the Iraqi government exam which marked the end of our intermediate studies and the elementary certificate of the French government.

That winter we became passionate newspaper readers. We breathlessly counted the allied victories. Now that Russia and America were fighting beside England, Hitler's fate was finally sealed.

Whenever Nessim talked about his discussions with Sereni, he took on the inspired look of someone listening to a far-off murmur. He did not dare believe in the reality of the foreign countries that were calling to him. He was fascinated by these lands that Sereni's voice evoked from the shadows.

Together, through novels and poems, we crossed the boundaries of different peoples and cultures. Countries subjugated by armies that wanted our defeat, our total annihilation. We waited for the ultimate victory that would open doors to the world for us and lift the threat that was hanging over our lives.

A month before the year-end Iraqi examinations, we wrote the examinations for the elementary certificate before a delegate sent by the French Ministry of Education. Students at the various Alliance schools or the Soeurs de la Présentation tested their first stammerings of French culture before Frenchmen.

That winter I had made three new discoveries: Gide, Malraux and Aragon. I was more than a little proud to be the only one who had received the precious message cast to the winds by these writers which, I was certain, had not been picked up by anyone else in Iraq.

In my talks with Nessim, I constantly evoked the authority of one or the other of my new masters. Gide launched a broad appeal, seizing our own destiny. Malraux's was the call to action — and to the reflection that must underlie every one of our acts.

Our energy was boundless. We were being crushed by a society that seemed increasingly oppressive, insensitive to our exaltations, to the driving power of our progress. We followed the exploits of the Chinese revolutionaries who were setting an example for us, accomplishing the action we only dreamed of.

I had read Aragon's *Le Crève-coeur*, published in Lebanon by the Free French. I translated parts of it into Arabic. His love of France matched my own, echoed it. My chosen country, which would satisfy all my desires, quench my insatiable thirst. France, wounded and besieged by barbarians, responded to my impatience to sing my own praises of that legendary land, free at last, opening its gates and its arms to those whose lips had tasted the wine of the West and now were waiting for the intoxication it would bring.

Lebanon and Syria had just escaped the authority of Vichy, and General de Gaulle's representatives were already in place. Free-French emissaries had come to supervise our French examinations.

As a composition topic, we were given a line in which Musset defended suffering. It was too good an opportunity not to quote Gide and Malraux. I was certain the examiner, even though he was French, had never heard of them. I felt that these writers must have had few readers aside from Nessim and me. And they would not dream of resuscitating Musset. As a precaution, I put the words "the famous contemporary French writer" after the names of Gide and Malraux, just as I did in my articles in Arabic newspapers.

In the notebook where we had to copy three poems we had learned by heart, I had given first place to Aragon's "les Lilas et les roses," followed by a poem by Baudelaire and, so as not to frighten the unknown examiner unduly, I had reserved a space for La Fontaine. In class we had mainly studied the *Fables*, with some timid incursions into the world of Lamartine and Victor Hugo.

I looked avidly at my examiner. He was the first Frenchman I had ever seen. This man was of the race of Molière and Baudelaire. I endowed him with magical powers.

Only later did I realize to what extent the oral examination had been one of the most decisive moments in my life. The French delegate, who seemed too young to be serious and who radiated a peculiarly occidental kind of good looks, asked me, without rolling his r's, to explain the Baudelaire poem to him. I could not do it. Patiently my examiner explained the meaning of the word "ostensoir" (monstrance). I discovered through his words that France concealed a thousand concrete details, that she had an everyday life and a religious tradition that escaped me completely, that no book had revealed to me yet. In Baghdad, where there was no one to contradict me, I had acquired an exclusive competence that no one questioned; and now in the presence of this Frenchman, I felt ignorant.

He was showing me that it was not enough to know the names of a few French writers and to read some of their books. The examiner did not seem to have noticed Aragon's poem. And with reason. He surely was completely unaware of the existence of his great compatriot. Otherwise he would have been struck by the homage I was paying to the singer of Free France, his own country. I turned the page of my notebook and stuck the page under his eyes, both hesitant and condescending.

"Yes, I saw that. It's a nice poem," he said, without the slightest surprise.

"You've heard of Aragon, have you?" I asked.

"Yes, of course," he said. "He's a friend of mine. But I haven't seen him for years."

What was he saying?

"Do you mean you actually know Aragon?"

"Yes, of course," he replied, laughing.

I held out my notebook with a trembling hand.

"Will you write your name here, please?"

He did so, in all seriousness. I forgot the examination, the poems, even Aragon himself. I was in the presence of a living representative of the kingdom inhabited by people whose names appeared on the first pages of French books. I was no longer listening to distant voices.

My classmates, who were waiting their turn, were growing impatient.

"Will you wait for me?" the Frenchman said. "I'll be finished in an hour and you could come to my hotel with me."

Suddenly Baghdad seemed to burst with a thousand new lights. This deserter from a world that was buried in books had a magical appeal for me. I could not even look at him. He was surrounded by the shadow of my exaltation. I listened to him complain about the oppressive heat.

We went to the Zia hotel and sat at a table on the terrace, beside the river.

"Ah, it's cooler here. Now I can breathe."

"Do you know any other writers?" I asked.

"A few. I teach literature and I'm a critic, so it's my job to know them."

"Where do you teach?"

"At the Ecole des Lettres in Beirut."

"Is it very hard to be admitted there?"

"No, although it would be too expensive for someone like you. You'd have your travelling expenses as well as your expenses in Beirut. You should go to Paris."

"Paris? But I'm Jewish, and the Germans …"

"The Germans won't be there forever. When France is liberated, she'll offer her culture to everyone. We'll give scholarships, like the United States and Great Britain.

"I read your composition," he went on. "I'd like to talk to you about it. You'll write to me, and I'll send you books. Maybe we'll arrange a scholarship."

The seed had been sown. From now on, I would not stop dreaming of my studies in Paris.

EIGHTEEN

THE FOLLOWING SUMMER, though Nessim and I had not yet reached the "age of reason" — the age required to enter government service — we found jobs elsewhere. Nessim was hired by his old director in the Censor's Bureau, who had just established an import–export company.

Thanks to my uncle's intervention, I was hired by a small Jewish bank with branches throughout the Middle East.

The bank's founder was a legendary figure. It was said that at the turn of the century, when he was foreign exchange agent on the Baghdad market, a Muslim who owed him money had fired at him point-blank, but missed. As his confidence in the protection the police might give him was far from certain, he decided to leave the country and set himself up in business in Beirut until his debtor had forgotten him.

The small business he founded in the country of his exile was transformed into a bank with branches in Damascus, Baghdad and finally in Alexandria and Cairo. He sent his numerous sons to universities in London and Paris so they could learn modern financial techniques, of whose subtleties he himself was ignorant.

Each branch was directed by a member of the family. Lacking a direct heir, he had placed his brother-in-law, in whom he did not have absolute confidence, at the head of the Baghdad branch. And every six months his eldest son, director of the Bank of Cairo, came to Baghdad to inspect his uncle's administration.

I was assigned to the correspondence and foreign relations department. My superior was a man who was still young but gave off a stifling odour of antiquity. He had been working for the establishment for fifteen years, starting when he was only sixteen.

From the beginning, he adopted a paternal attitude towards me. I resembled him, he said. I was starting out at the same age as he. Even though our relationship was marked by warmth and cordiality, I was terrified whenever I imagined myself in his place fifteen years later. I kept telling him that I was going to continue my education and had no intention of ending my days in a bank.

He dictated letters to me in English and French, leaving me free to write the Arabic letters myself. He declared with no false shame or modesty that he was uncertain of some of the grammatical subtleties of our mother tongue.

He gradually assigned me all of the correspondence, contenting himself with guiding me and supervising my work.

There was constant activity in our office. Importers, exporters, tourists, fathers sending allowances to their student sons in Lebanon or Egypt. Our rates were better than any of the competing banks, and our services gave the appearance of bonhomie and familiarity.

The world of entertainment had a prize position among our clients. Cinema owners paid the producers of Egyptian films through us, and this entitled us to free tickets in the leading theatres. We were also visited by touring Lebanese or Egyptian stars who were sending part of their hard-earned money home. Each time one of the female stars crossed the doorstep, the whole bank succumbed to her spell.

Female singers and dancers who passed the counters gave off a dense perfume which temporarily dissipated the rancid odour of sweat that was dried by ceiling fans. When one of them appeared, the director would begin to fuss and fidget, asserting the importance of his position. Under the most futile pretexts, he would come to our office, smiling at the lady, showing by the way he interrogated my supervisor that he was master. He would sniff at her perfume and stare at her as avidly and insistently as an adolescent.

These women knew how to speak to men besides their brothers or husbands without giggling like children. And they did not affect the coarse laughter and gestures of prostitutes. Associating with men was part of their work and they had learned to use their charms without being ostentatious.

The director would greet them with much bowing of the head and gestures of obeisance. He succeeded only in looking ridiculous. The stars would model their own gestures on his, and they would emphasize their airs and affect aristocratic poses.

One day an Egyptian singer, Laila, who had been in Baghdad for four or five years and was one of the most frequently seen "artistes," came into our office, greeted my superior courteously and sat down next to me. Surprised and embarrassed, my superior chose to ignore this unwonted scene. Lowering his eyes, he diligently returned to work as though nothing had happened. Although it did not appear so, the bank was in a state of commotion.

Two years earlier, I had seen Laila sing and dance at the marriage of the daughter of one of my mother's cousins and I had secretly admired her ever since.

When Laila appeared, the guests greeted her with deafening applause. She went directly to a room where she stayed for several minutes. Finally she burst from the shadows, decked out in brilliant colours. A skirt split up the middle revealed the brown tones of her smooth skin. Her naked belly was offered to our view and her generous bosom, squeezed into imitation pearls and diamonds, was tossed about in rhythm with her steps. In a few seconds she was turning to the sound of the orchestra which had stopped abruptly to emphasize her entry into the room. Men, women and children hung on each of her gestures, panting with impatience as they waited for the voice that would soon tear through the silence.

She started with a Ya Laili. She improvised soft, delicate tones. Peacefully, with studied slowness, she seemed to be containing herself before abandonment. At first no one was prepared to follow her. Then, imperceptibly, she silenced all our resistance. Soon she would lead us into the whirlwind of her emotions and her wild imprecations. She was silent. She had started the movement and now she stopped. She was testing her own strength. Cries burst out: *Allah, Allah.* Applause resounded. With half-tones, the *oud* surrendered to a hesitant and muted music. The silence had barely been broken and the *oud* reminded us that the mystery was many-sided. Laila resumed her invocation of the night. At the slightest interruption of her singing, the orchestra would take up the melody. Laila was standing, motionless, completely alone. Rigid, hands on her hips, her voice rose, stretched out, spread. The spiralling cry resounded in a thousand echoes. We held our breath. We were puppets and she held the strings. The rhythm made her our omnipotent ruler. Suddenly, everything stopped. It was the end and it was signalled by an outburst. Free, relieved, an explosion of cries and applause translated our exaltation. Then she gave way to a popular song. We sang along with her, although we were content just to move our lips, humming, so as not to lose the modulations of a voice whose perfection gave nobility to the most common tunes.

Now this woman, this great Egyptian star, was sitting beside me. I inhaled her perfume. She had a favour to ask me, hoped I could be discreet. She held a piece of paper in her hand. She looked around her. My imagination raced. My superior was still bent over a pile of papers and seemed completely absorbed in his work.

"This letter came today," she said, "and I can't read it without my glasses. Will you read it to me?"

She was frail, humble, stripped of power. Without her magic mask, the protection of distance, she lost her aura.

In childish handwriting, the letter began, "Dear Mama." The girl wrote that she was in good health, was going to school and her father was taking good care of her. He had bought her a new dress and taken her to the movies. He said it was expensive and the money she had sent had quickly evaporated. He asked for more. She sent a kiss and signed the letter "Salima."

Laila thanked me. Moved at first, she then became angry. "You'd think he has holes in his hands," she said. "He just gets my cheque and already he's asking for more."

She hesitated, looked around, watching the director's office.

"I'm going to abuse your kindness. I'm going to ask you to write a few lines for me."

"Of course," I replied, recovering the spirit of chivalry proper to the man who must abandon forever any dream of adventure.

"My dear daughter," she began. She advised her daughter to eat well, study hard. Soon she would send more money to her father but he would have to restrain his impulsive spending and be more discerning. "We must beware of those who assure us of their friendship. Often they're only hypocrites who take advantage of our gullibility and weave dark plots behind our backs." This mixture of loyal sentiments and advice, of which I was the interpreter, ended with the words, "Your loving mother."

She was overwhelmed with gratitude. She didn't know how to thank me. But yes, she knew exactly what to do, because she invited me to go to hear her at the nightclub. Tickets would be available for me on whatever evening I wanted. And so as not to annoy my superior, who must have heard every word of our conversation, she invited him to join me. He protested for the sake of form.

"No, I insist," she said. "You must both come. It will make me happy."

He arranged an evening for the two of us.

My colleagues clustered around me. What a chance to become the lover of a woman who does not dispense her charms on account. The bank director was filled with concern for me.

"Son, don't let yourself get carried away by that kind of woman."

My disappointment grew keener. What a bad melodrama I had become involved in! The goddess of song was illiterate. How could I reconcile my image of the artiste adulated by newspapers, celebrated by a delirious public, with this poor weeping mother? Neither the story of a husband living off his wife, nor the artiste who must submit to the shameful exploitation of an unscrupulous man, could touch my sensibility.

The next evening, I went reluctantly to the nightclub with my superior. It was summer and the performance was given outside. Most of the people sitting around the tables wore the *akal*. The sheiks were vacationing in Baghdad, their wives sheltered from the glances of the indiscreet. The artistes reserved other delights for them besides the pleasures of sight and sound. Already, some were entertaining their clients with glasses of *arak*.

When Laila made her entrance, she moved straight ahead, proud, aloof. Unlike the others, she lived only for her art and never sat at the table with her customers. It was whispered that this was only a trick to raise her prices. She stopped at our table. She lingered, sitting on the edge of a chair. She greeted us warmly, like a hostess welcoming guests in her own house. Then turning to me she said, "What song would you like to hear?"

I told her. The song she had sung the night of the wedding. But now its charm was broken.

My superior was certain that Laila was in love with me, despite my vehement denials.

"You don't seem to realize how lucky you are. There are sheiks who would pay thirty, forty dinars to have Laila sit at their table."

And without moving a finger, I had something that was worth twice my monthly salary.

NINETEEN

IN THE SUMMER my brother's day began at dawn. He would leap out of bed at the first rays of light and before leaving the roof he would shake my bed.

"Time to get up."

Several friends rented a boat for the season when the weather turned hot. Every morning before going to work, we would meet three or four of them. We wore our bathing suits under our clothes, and as soon as we were in the boat we were ready to jump in the water. Swimming was more than a sport, it was a ritual. Between daybreak and the first rays of sun, we defied the blinding light and unbearable heat for an hour, at leisure and with impunity. My brother never left the water without swimming across the Tigris in both directions. I accompanied him, always a few lengths behind. The lazier athletes followed us from the comfort of the boat. Winded by fatigue, I would look enviously at them. As I went under the bridge, I'd hold onto a pillar to catch my breath.

"Are you tired?" my brother would ask.

"Not at all," I'd protest and set off again.

We reached the other shore with the first rays of the sun. There was no question of lingering on the sand, strewn with stones and objects that had been thrown out of nearby windows and balconies. We had to consider the sun which would soon be striking hard. Swimming back, we would just have time to go home for breakfast before leaving for the office.

At the end of the afternoon when the sun was retreating, my brother often repeated the crossing in the lukewarm water. He could not persuade me to join him.

I would go and sit in a café near the house, applying myself as earnestly as I could to making my entry into Iraqi literature.

I often met Nessim at the café, surrounded by his books, newspapers and notebooks. He was travelling as seriously as I was down the road of dreams and self-expression. We read avidly. Surrounded by people playing backgammon and dominoes, we would give in sometimes to the pleasure of argument, passionate examinations of questions, enthusiasms, even disappointments. Speared by the imperious demands of time, we could feel the moments weighing on us. They were precious and must not be dispersed in useless chatter. Books were the source of life for us. We discovered the full and radiant existence of Europeans and realized how bare our own lives were, how stifling the limits of our surroundings.

The evenings slowly released us from the crushing heat of the day. The coolness invited us to a certain levity.

"Let's go for a walk," one of us would say.

We would plunge into Abou Nawass Street as into a private domain. On the benches, men, women — most of them veiled — and sometimes children would spend the evening watching the river. Every day we would measure our space and our solitude.

We watched the river flow. Dirty, it sometimes carried the carcass of a donkey or a dog. It proclaimed itself from a distance, in the dark, by the odour which we avoided by holding our noses.

At the height of summer, a small island appeared in the middle of the low river water. *Chardaghs*, little huts made of braided rushes, were built on it. All summer we would light fires for cooking fish on this ephemeral land.

At the sound of the *oud* and the singing, boats would draw up around the island. Jews and Christians would bring their wives, sisters and sometimes their mothers and aunts, but the Muslim men came alone.

Twice a month my brother had the boat to himself for the evening. Then the whole family would go to the *jazra*, the island, for a feast of *masgouf*, grilled fish. During the day, my mother would prepare tomatoes and gherkins that would season the two or three fish we would devour. All together we would dip our fingers into the warm tender flesh. But these were fleeting, isolated pleasures that did not make up for our painful need for woman. Now we were waiting for a future that would be more than reading and dreams.

TWENTY

THE ALLIANCE CLASSES stopped at the *moutawassita,* the intermediate level, and we needed two years of secondary studies in order to graduate and attend university. We could choose between a scientific and a literary course. What doors would the literary course open to a Jew? Our classmates wasted no time looking for the answer: they all chose the science option. They did not want to be forced into the fine vocation of schoolteacher and offer new evidence of loyalty to the Arab nation.

Nessim and I were obsessed with chemistry, physics, algebra and geometry. But when examination time was near, we took pleasure in reviewing grammar, rereading literary texts and plunging once again into Arabic history. We never tired of discovering the rhetorical wealth of our language and we enjoyed repeating the words, rewriting the sentences of our great writers, thereby declaring our own virtuosity in handling the whole range of its unique music.

The foreign books we read accentuated our intimacy with Arabic words and nourished our love for our own very special melodies. We were eager to share our enthusiasm and the fruits of our discoveries with newspaper and magazine readers. We were committed to the noble and uplifting task of serving our culture and our language.

Most of our classmates had enrolled in the Shamash School, which prepared them for the Iraqi government examinations and allowed them to try the matriculation examinations that would be given by the delegates from the University of London.

As I knew what I wanted to do, I decided not to try for the British diploma. Besides, Nessim and I wanted to keep our jobs and were forced to continue our studies at night, so the Shamash School was out of the question. There was a Jewish school that gave evening courses, but only in science. So we had no choice: we enrolled in a Muslim school.

"You'll have to learn whole pages of the Koran by heart," our classmates said, half mocking. "You'll have to explain all the poetry of the Jahiliyah."

Of course our problems with Arabic were not over, with its archaic words that had fallen into disuse and others whose meaning had changed. None of our classmates dared to state openly his secret thoughts: that it was useless for a Jew.

We chose a school with the best pedagogical guarantees and which was recognized as one of the high spots of Muslim traditionalism and Arab nationalism. Every evening we took the same route through the dark and winding streets of Heyderkhana, going around the Great Mosque. We sat on the same bench, staying close to one another in our difference. We were the only Jews in the class, and we did not expect friendship. On the contrary, we feared outright hostility. Most of the students were functionaries hoping for promotions to better positions.

Our teacher had a keen awareness of the linguistic and grammatical mystery of the Koran and of pre-Islamic poetry. We delighted in this endless discovery of our cultural past. For it was our past: no reservation, no restriction, crossed our minds. In our writers' dreams, our attempts at self-expression, we borrowed the words used by the prophet Mohammed to transcribe the word of God as it had been transmitted to the angel Gabriel. We struggled with the same words as our predecessors, desert knights or dwellers of palaces. We trembled at the successes of our elders, shuddered with admiration for the images and rhymes of Al Maarri and Al Mutannabbi. More than the caliphs who had paid them, more than the masters of the day, they were the true conquerors and their victories remained eternally alive.

We soon realized that our blind enthusiasm, our frantic love for the masters whose heirs we claimed to be, were not shared by our classmates. And it was that admirable interpreter of the millenary message of unalterable beauty, our literature teacher, who most objected to our enthusiasm. He would question the whole class about a grammatical ambiguity or a complicated figure of speech. Nessim and I were usually among the first to raise our hands, pointing out with joy that we held the key to the mystery. The teacher never called on us. He persisted in ignoring our eagerness to declare our attachment to our common heritage and unconsciously rejected the tribute we were burning to pay to his teaching.

Once, Nessim was the only volunteer in a desert of ignorance and silence. He raised his hand. The teacher, who could not push his objection to that point, gestured. In a trembling voice, Nessim gave the answer, but the teacher merely told him to sit down.

The next day we were the only ones who knew the meaning of a verse from the Koran. Nessim raised his hand timidly, then lowered it. He nudged me with his elbow, urging me on. The teacher stared at me, looked at my raised hand and, without faltering, concluded, "So, no one has put up his hand."

One night as we were about to take our places on the usual bench, we found that it was occupied. We went to the next one, when a student told us it was reserved. This was repeated several times. Swallowing our humiliation, we went to a completely empty bench. The next day we arrived before the others and took our usual places. Counting on his rights as a conqueror, the student who had taken our places the night before ordered us to leave. Speaking through clenched lips, I told Nessim not to move. The boy, who worked in the passport office, was tall and thin, with a small black moustache the only source of interest on his narrow face. He squinted and his little black eyes were almost imperceptible in their deep sockets. Storming with rage, he began to insult us. The other students, waiting for something to happen, enjoyed themselves in silence. Nessim and I chatted, trying to appear completely unaware of the others. The student's threats became more violent as he promised to break our bones.

Two other students intervened. Laughing at us, they begged him to take pity on the weak.

TWENTY-ONE

WE WERE CONTINUING to discover western literature but our true occupation, a painful one that secretly underlay all our conversations, was woman. Some evenings, when a number of us were together, we would indulge in a round of boasting and imaginary adventures. None of us believed the incredible conquests, even less the detailed accounts of erotic performances. But there was always the hope that one day these pursuits would be realized. We promised ourselves that we would spend our lives in adulation of beautiful and loving women and the intimacy of sumptuous nuptial couches whose delights would always remain.

Those who frequented houses of prostitution transposed their sexual exploits into sublime adventures, ornamenting them with all their repressed sentimentality, clothing them in romanticism. Images of famous lovers in novels prolonged their brief visits to the neighbourhood prostitutes.

When the time came for Nessim and me to join the game, Nessim took malicious pleasure in breaking the spell. He would exaggerate so much that the dream would crumble. Then we would put one another off with coarse jokes and vulgar laughter. We would laugh at our adventures, uncertain of our own sexual abilities. Often it would end badly and the jokes would turn to insults.

We carefully avoided talking about real love. It was too ephemeral and precious to serve as fuel for the others' scorn, and it would seem pale in comparison with accounts of imaginary prowess.

When winter was over, our neighbours hired a maid, a Kurdish Jew who had just arrived from Zakho, a city whose inhabitants were known for their strength and appetite for hard work. They provided the best laundresses, porters and maids. The new servant, who was sixteen or seventeen, always wore soiled dresses that were torn, allowing a glimpse of her thigh. When I walked past the door, which was often partly open, I stared at her hungrily. Sometimes I would see her on the roof, leaning on the balustrade or hanging out the clothes she had just washed.

There was no disguise in my famished eyes, but her status as a domestic forbade her to sound the alarm for her honour. She showed her bare arms without embarrassment, a unique gift of a femininity that was buried under veils. One day she stared at me with her large black eyes, and the next day I thought I could detect the beginning of a smile. She was standing in the doorway. I turned around. I smiled at her, causing such an unexpected reaction that my heart began to pound; she offered me a smile that showed her dazzling teeth. The sign was undeniable. The next day she leaned against the door, offering another smile, a new declaration. I could not contain my joy.

The adventure grew in my mind from hour to hour. I pushed aside anything that might dampen my enthusiasm. Illiterate? Yes, but intelligence redeems ignorance. And her beauty? There was a risk of passing to one side if one only lingered over appearances. Once she was washed and made up, properly dressed, she would triumph over the fabulous heroines of western novels.

Whenever I reached the curve in the street, I would be seized with anticipation. Would she be there? In front of the door, on the roof or in the corridor? Perhaps I would meet her on the street, coming home from market.

Sometimes when her employer was nearby, giving her instructions, I would go past, feigning not to know her.

Her name, Sarah, was clothed in all the beauty and authenticity of Judaism and the East. She was a girl who was not ashamed of her origins but displayed them proudly. No, she would not let herself be adorned with a western name like Valentine, Espérance or Angèle. I would avenge her. I would praise her beauty in poems dedicated to her. But a shadow slipped into this serene landscape and slowed me down; she would not be able to read my poems.

One day when I was coming home from work, I saw her at the bus stop, half hidden behind the porch of a house at the top of our street. She was waiting for me. The noon sun did not invite passersby to linger. They went on their way, impatient to take off their clothes in the coolness of their houses.

With a lump in my throat, I walked rapidly to control the trembling of my legs. When I was two steps away from Sarah, I turned my head. No one was nearby. The time had come to act like a man. With my most dazzling smile, I stared at her and stammered, "How are you?"

Without a sign of embarrassment, she replied happily, in the best Kurdish accent, "I'm fine." But she wasn't going to stop there. She wanted to show that she could take the initiative, play her part in building this fine love story. She added hastily, "It's hot out," and ran off towards her employer's house.

It was up to me to pursue this first encounter, but there was no lack of obstacles. First, how could one continue the conversation without alerting the whole street? If only she could read, I would have written her the plans for our next rendezvous and told her of my feelings.

Two days later Sarah was again waiting for me at the bus stop. This time I was not satisfied with banalities. As soon as I saw her, I walked directly towards her, and boldly, my mind fully made up, I said, "What's your name?"

Feeling vaguely apprehensive, I measured the power of feminine coquetry.

"Don't you know? It's Sarah. I know your name and I think it's nice."

She waited a few seconds. Realizing that our conversation was not going to continue, she walked away.

My secret joy was gradually transformed into concern. Would I let such an opportunity slip by? But what should I do? Sarah had one day off every week, and perhaps we could arrange to meet. But where?

I knew that some men, usually older than I, had mistresses: maids, sometimes nurses. They rented rooms in *maisons de passe* for their secret meetings. The wealthier ones would get together, four or five of them, to rent a house which they would take turns using. Their mistresses were not unselfish lovers. They were more expensive than admitted prostitutes. Moreover, nurses and maids soon learned to enjoy their new station; and urged on by the owners of the suspicious houses where they isolated themselves with their lovers, they finally became regular tenants.

The inevitable road of vice took shape before me like some terrifying threat. Was I going to lead a young girl, innocent and beautiful, who spontaneously offered me her heart and her love, along the road of perdition? Could I ever forgive myself?

What should I do? Sarah would only laugh at the poems

she had inspired. In her mind, a real man would not delay. He would act.

The next day Sarah was at our usual meeting place at the bus stop. Without looking at me, without seeming to know me, she walked past me and, not even seeming to speak to me, said, "I love you," and went on her way.

Just what did she want? An affair, of that there was no doubt. I was dreaming about that too. Ah, the delights of a night of murmuring and caresses. Of course I would have to cut them short to put myself at her level. She even spoke Arabic with a Kurdish accent and her "I love you," so laden with emotion, was slightly ridiculous.

I refrained from talking to anyone about it. I did not even take Nessim into my confidence, fearing that some day he would treat my love affair as a big joke.

I didn't know where to go beyond a smile. Sarah had made up her mind and abandoned the struggle. Her smiles became absent-minded, distant and increasingly rare. She no longer sought furtive meetings, but rather avoided them. Obviously I was unable to act like a man. She would leave me to serve my apprenticeship.

As soon as this adventure had ended, it gave way to another. One of the neighbours used to stand at her window at dusk. Reading or knitting, she would nonchalantly watch the passersby. She was beautiful, at least she seemed so to me. I knew her brother vaguely and always greeted him when I saw him, hoping in this way to come closer to his sister's heart. To her I would give bold and insistent looks. She did not look away and I considered that an encouragement.

Tired of this sign language whose effectiveness was not guaranteed, I resolved to take the first step and pay honour to my identity as a man. I wrote a letter telling her of my passion.

I urged her to reply immediately and not be afraid to mail her answer. No one would open my personal mail. I kept the letter in my pocket, having decided to give it to her at the first opportunity.

For months the letter remained in my billfold. Two or three times I passed her in the street but it never seemed the right moment to hand it to her.

TWENTY-TWO

VICTIMS OF A perpetual state of agitation, some of us took refuge in political action and postponed the discoveries to be made when bodies came together in shared voluptuousness. We were going to change society and hasten the advent of a world where we could freely pick the fruits of love. We would have our revenge in the end. We would crush the blind society that refused us the joys that were lavished without constraint under other skies.

Of course at the first sign of desire, our families would, with great care and circumspection, arrange a marriage that would put an end to our fast. We were not yet reduced to such submission. After so much crying and howling, we could show that we were patient. And then to what excesses would we not go to reconcile our reading and writing with a reality that was so dry. We would condemn ourselves to perpetual exile, and that would be the end of our dreams.

One evening Nessim's remarks about women were more eloquent than usual. He seemed haughty and displayed the tranquil assurance of one who holds the key to the mystery. At length, he became more precise: as soon as you begin to associate with women, you stop surrounding them with fictitious splendours.

"You're absolutely right," I said. "Women are flesh-and-blood creatures just like us."

But he was not going to stop when he was doing so well.

"You know, you can only find out what women are really like in bed."

His game of hide-and-seek was irritating me.

"We don't usually talk in riddles. If you've got something to tell me, don't go around in circles."

I understood that if he was putting on the airs of a man of experience, it was to conceal his shame. Along with a colleague from the office, he had gone to a house that guaranteed everything, including clean girls.

"The experience would be marvellous if you could only leave out the place and the circumstances," he said.

Had he been unable to close his eyes to the hideous details? It was a shock, but it happened to everyone the first time. Next time he would overcome his shyness and prejudice, because he firmly intended to continue his visits. And in a rather timid voice, he said, "You could come with me if you want."

Had we not promised never to drink that water? How often had we cursed the Gemonies and promised to fight for enlightened public opinion, to castigate those responsible for the shameful practices, unworthy merchants of human flesh? Was there a worse degradation of woman and love? Yet there we were, ready to set aside principles and indignation, becoming accomplices in this sordid traffic.

THE NIGHT OF OUR VISIT, Nessim took childlike pleasure in playing the role of guide.

"Here's the synagogue. The house is just two steps away. Here we are," he added in a low voice.

We walked along the sombre street as though we were hatching some plot. The house seemed completely sunk into darkness.

We were not afraid, because mystery was part of the décor. This *maison de passe*, like the dozens of others scattered through every part of town, from the most elegant to the most miserable, functioned illegally. Not that prostitution was forbidden, but it was authorized only in the section set aside for it, the Maydane, where everything took place under the watchful eye of the police and Health Department inspectors. But the Maydane was the last refuge of the prostitutes who could no longer find customers in brothels. Most had some infirmity or were past retirement age.

The clandestine houses were only invisible to those passersby who did not want to see them. The residents of the neighbourhood knew they existed, as their own rent was reduced because of the proximity of these bastions of vice. The police gave their protection in return for certain compensations. Nothing disturbed the habitual silence of the alley and there was no outward sign to mark the house of pleasure.

Nessim walked up. As party to the secret, he did not ring the bell but knocked at the door three times. Our eyes grew accustomed to the dark, and we could see a low window that opened onto a darkened room. A cigarette, like a shooting star, cut through the dense shadows.

"Who are you?" a man asked us in the finest Muslim accent.

Attempting to use the same accent, Nessim replied, "Is Abou Hassan here?"

The door was opened. "Come in quickly."

And the *kawad* who received us led us down a dimly lit corridor into the reception room. Dazzled by the sudden brightness, we could distinguish two men smoking. Judging by their clothes, they were functionaries or small businessmen. The *kawad*, like all pimps, exhibited two gold teeth, a big ring, a full moustache, and carefully slicked-down black hair. He did not give up his

Muslim accent even though no one had any illusions about it. We were all Jewish. But as soon as we crossed the threshold of the house, we changed our identities. In this exotic land, the Jewish accent would seem out of place. Speaking an adopted language, we could carry on only simple business negotiations and any embarrassment would be superfluous. With our new faces, we would become unknown.

"Do you wish someone in particular?" asked the *kawad.*

"Yes. Samirah," Nessim answered for me.

"She isn't free. This gentleman is waiting for her too."

He pointed to one of our two companions. The man, impassive, did not show the least embarrassment.

"And you?" he asked Nessim.

"I'll see, I haven't decided yet."

The second customer smoked as he kept crossing and uncrossing his legs. As the *kawad* left the room, he soothed him, saying, "Najiba will be free soon."

Then we heard him knock on a door and shout, "Najiba, hurry up, somebody's waiting for you."

Two tenants made a noisy entrance. The *kawad* stood in the entry and jerked his chin at Nessim. He was the recalcitrant one who had to submit. They wore only peignoirs that did not even conceal the attributes of their femininity. Outrageously made up, they gave off a strong scent of roses. One of the two, slightly older than her companion, went towards Nessim and as a greeting placed her hand on his manhood.

With an air of complicity, she looked at her companion who had a tattooed nose; like all prostitutes, she was proud of her dazzling row of gold teeth which she exhibited every time she burst out into coarse laughter.

"He says he doesn't know who he wants, but I know."

And she presented the evidence. Nessim was blushing. Everything was happening so quickly that I could not seize the thread of events. I was in the presence of woman, so much desired, so long lusted over. With no hint of modesty or hesitation, she offered to fulfil our most unspeakable desires.

Nessim uttered little cries and sharp laughter like a child being tickled. If he did not want to obey and follow his assailant, it was because he was waiting for me to be served first. And directing the attention of the women to me, he announced, "It's his first time."

The assailant relaxed. She had not been asked to look after me. But she would repair the oversight.

"We'll take care of your friend ... Fahima!" she called to her companion, and with her eyes commanded her to release me from my solitude.

Fahima obeyed and came closer to me. Smaller and thinner than her friend, Fahima's technique was more appropriate to her stature. Without having time to notice it, I could feel Fahima crushing me beneath her weight. Although she sat on my knees, her feet touched the ground and she was leaning so that she could rub herself against me. For the first time, a woman was touching me. She brought her head close to mine and our cheeks touched.

"Don't wait for Samirah. I'm better than she is. Come with me, you'll see."

Despite the essence of roses, she gave off such a strong smell of onions that I managed to forget that woman, the painful mystery, had finally found her place on my knees. And with a certain victorious male satisfaction, I rejected her insistent advances.

"No, I'm waiting for Samirah," I said disdainfully.

Two new visitors appeared in the doorway. Before they had time to sit down, the hostesses were clinging to their necks and the two couples vanished into the hallway arm in arm.

Nessim's smile was smug and satisfied, as though all his predictions were being confirmed.

Coming up to me, he whispered triumphantly, "I had her. She gave me a little extra for nothing."

Was he entering so quickly into the game, accepting the rules?

At last it was my turn. Nessim, still filled with solicitude, stood between Samirah and me. Protectively, he said, "I put him in your hands. This is his first time."

Samirah took my hand and led me to her room. Scarcely furnished, the bed dominated. The dark cover, threadbare around the edges, did not look too dirty. Two wooden chairs stood against the wall. A few large nails to hang clothes on. A soiled mirror.

At the foot of the bed there was a basin, a copper jug and a bar of soap.

"Do you want a safe?" Samirah asked before I had time to look at her. Panic-stricken, I examined the rudimentary furniture.

"A safe? Yes, of course."

Without opening the door she shouted, "Nouri, bring me a safe."

Nouri was the man-of-all-work. He was fifteen or sixteen. As he held the prophylactic out to me, he was establishing contact so that I would not forget him when the tips were being given out.

"I changed the water in the pitcher," he told me.

It was then that Samirah looked directly at me. Now we were alone.

"Is this really your first time?" she asked me, incredulous.

"Yes," I confessed.

"You have to get undressed," she instructed me. And to lighten my task she added, "You don't have to take off everything."

Having decided to do things properly, I removed everything.

She lay on the bed. I came over to her, and she kissed my

cheek. She was so young and she smelled of soap. It was my turn to play. Would I be able to accomplish my task? Wanting to put off the moment, I tried to gain some time.

"How about you, aren't you getting undressed?" I asked.

"Usually it costs more if I get undressed. I won't charge you anything, but don't tell Salim."

She was naked. Never in all my dreams had I imagined a woman so resplendent in her beauty, so filled with poetry. I held out my hand towards her, timidly, touched one breast, then the other. She laughed to encourage me and then began to stare at my impassive virility.

"It's always a problem the first time," she consoled.

She held me in her arms, caressed me. Everything happened at a cadence that took my breath away. It was as though she had burst out of a dream, like a phantom. I held her close, caressed her arms, her legs, her thighs.

"Lie down," she said and pushed me onto the bed. "I'll get on top of you."

My joy vanished and was transformed into fear. Failure was lying in wait for me and, afterwards, mockery and laughter. And the time allotted to me was passing. Salim, the *kawad*, was growing impatient, and he rapped at the door.

"Hurry up, Samirah, people are waiting for you."

Samirah was filled with compassion and apologies.

"He's going to think we've done it twice and he'll make you pay double."

I felt as though I were dissolving and shrinking. Samirah was so beautiful, but it was evanescent. I didn't even have time to satisfy my eyes. Ah, if only we could be alone, with no intruders; without a jug or soap, without being called to order. If only I could speak to her, tell her my name, ask her age.

"Are you from Baghdad?" I asked with the Jewish accent.

"I come from Karbala. My father is a mullah," she said in the purest Muslim accent.

We both burst out laughing. The joke was the first real contact between us. We were accomplices, but too late.

"You'll have to leave now, but come back and see me and I'll tell you the story of my life."

Her tone was both mocking and motherly.

I got dressed. The pimp knew of my failure. I gave him what I owed, my chin low, staring into space. He apologized for making me pay for goods I had not been able to claim but which had been completely at my disposal.

"Come in the morning next time. You can stay longer."

I avoided Nessim's look and, crestfallen, went outside with him. He understood. He had had the same experience, he assured me. He had also found himself short of desire. But I stopped listening to him. How could I implore him not to tell anyone of my shameful performance? Then I was struck by a more painful concern. What if I never succeeded in acting like a man?

Next morning, when the offices opened, I was at Samirah's door. I had told my supervisor I was sick. I drew the *kawad* aside.

"Don't knock at the door. I'll pay double, even triple, but leave us alone."

Samirah was already familiar to me and she gave me the treatment of a regular customer. In a few minutes the proof was rendered. I passed the test successfully, but with no witness. There was no one to attest to my victory. Samirah did not spare her praise. Triumphantly I examined her body like an inanimate object. Already I had rediscovered my solitude.

TWENTY-THREE

PROOF HASTILY GIVEN in the intimacy of brothels, with uncertain conclusions, no longer satisfied me in my attempts to demonstrate my masculinity. I wanted assurance and I needed consolation. When my sister became engaged, I had the opportunity to make my man's voice resound, but no one asked for my advice, particularly the primary interested party. The voice had to be content with its echo. But the words it pronounced had the unsuspected virtue of giving me the illusion of power while discharging me of any real responsibility.

My sister was about to turn twenty-four. The family was very concerned. If they weren't careful, she would slip imperceptibly into the ranks of old maids. She would lose one of the first qualities demanded by marriage candidates: her youth. No one in the family devalued her needlessly by admitting that she was already past twenty. Whenever my grandmother suspected that she had an interested listener, she would keep repeating that my sister had just turned eighteen. My mother contradicted her several times, declaring with great concern for accuracy that my sister was eighteen and a half, she was "growing," and that for her as for the rest of mankind, the years were passing quickly. But these tricks fooled only those who were indifferent. Anyone who was interested could make inquiries, uncovering any subterfuge. He could discover within a few weeks the date on which his intended had first seen the light of day.

To provide for any eventuality, the best *dellals* were charged with listing my sister among their candidates. Qualities: young, beautiful, excellent education, fine family, magnificent health, admirable character. Conditions: no debts, trousseau to be discussed.

A young girl was offered to a boy only when his parents had expressed their agreement in principle to the union of the two families, after making inquiries. If refused, she risked seeing her chances decrease. The girl was always blamed for her failure. If the motives were not obvious, mysterious reasons were imagined that no one dared reveal so as not to needlessly harm the poor girl's reputation.

The *dellal* submitted a list with the names of six possible candidates. Three were rejected out of hand by my mother and my uncle: the age difference was far too great. One of the postulants had been twenty years old when my sister was born. The second came from a rather disreputable family, although it was very rich; one of his cousins lived as a concubine with a Christian. The third had a modest income and seemed to have little chance of progress in his profession, school teaching.

The contest to judge the respective merits of the other three began. Everyone was asked to contribute: my brother knew the cousin of the first one, my uncle knew the uncle of the second one, and I knew his nephew.

My sister was present at all the deliberations, but only as an observer, never participating — because of shyness but also because she knew the limits of her role and the place she was allowed in the deliberations. She gave her opinion only when two candidates were of equal merit. Finally, the choice fell to a man named Sasson, a cloth merchant who had a shop in the Souk. An honourable family, with no tuberculosis or mental illness, and no prostitute among its members. Average income, acceptable character, satisfying. He was not known to have any vices or mistresses. Age: rather advanced, although the gap was not excessive.

"Is he handsome?" my sister asked.

The question was deemed appropriate.

"He isn't ugly," my uncle answered discreetly.

My grandmother opened the debate.

"A man's beauty is in his money and his character."

My sister was not satisfied. She insisted, "Is he intelligent?"

My grandmother had an answer for everything.

"How else could he have such a fine position?"

The day of the first visit, my mother and sister veiled themselves from head to toe and went incognito to Sasson's boutique. Disguised as ordinary customers, they bargained at length, without buying anything.

When they came home my sister remarked, "He's short and very dark."

"He has a small nose and his features are very delicate," my mother corrected her. "Your children wouldn't have big noses or mouths."

"His eyes are small," my sister went on.

"They're bright," my mother retorted.

My sister, who did not have a broad choice, and who was terrified at the prospect of staying at home for another year, was not really unhappy. She had never liked school. She knew she was not gifted for study. In any case, education was really intended only for boys. Girls were expected to get married.

Her husband would not be made in the image of the chivalrous men who broke women's hearts in American and Egyptian films, but he would have the advantage of being a known quantity. She would have her own house, furniture, dishes, perhaps a maid. What more could she ask?

Meanwhile, Sasson had also proceeded to carry out a scrupulous inquiry and he wanted to see at closer range the woman who might share his bed for the rest of his days. As my sister no longer went to school, she could not be taken by surprise on her way out of class. For the first meeting, a public place was chosen, the Al Sadoun Park. Everything would follow a rigorous plan. Accompanied by my mother, Sasson would walk innocently through the park. He would go past my sister and inspect her directly. My sister would get up and walk slowly towards the exit; and he would be able to watch how she walked, her figure, examine her legs, her back.

My sister felt as though she were trying another final examination, and that took away all her pleasure.

"It's very important," I warned her. "It will change your life."

"I know," she answered.

My grandmother did not spare her own advice.

"And most important, when you laugh, be careful not to show your big teeth. Don't open your mouth when you smile."

"Yes, yes," she answered. She couldn't wait for the ordeal to be over.

As soon as the meeting had taken place, the *dellal* hastened to announce the good news: Sasson was satisfied. The first stage was complete; other more serious questions had to be settled. The matter would not be concluded until an agreement had been reached on the material conditions for the union.

Sasson delegated his father for these negotiations. Ordinarily my father would have represented my sister, but the family agreed to assign this task to my uncle, whose judgement and savoir-faire were greater than my father's.

Our first condition was accepted: no dowry. My sister's beauty entitled her to such a privilege. Then we had to agree on the size of a trousseau. In addition to a complete set of furniture for an entire house, Sasson's father demanded linen, clothing and silver cutlery. This was the obstacle that blocked the spokesmen temporarily. My mother, prepared to sell all her jewels for the trousseau and the ceremony, did not want to go into debt for the silver. The *dellal* intervened. The angles were smoothed out. Sasson would have only two silver vases.

On the great day, my sister wore a white silk gown with large red flowers. Her makeup made her look as though she were trying to erase all trace of freshness from her face. She found many things to do, thereby avoiding useless talk. Was she concealing her joy out of shyness, or was she trying to put her pain to rest and forget her sorrow? She prepared for the ceremony as though she did not have the leading role.

As was fitting on such occasions, my future brother-in-law was an hour late. He was flanked by a battalion of relatives: brothers, sisters, brothers-in-law and sisters-in-law. All eyes were on him but he did not seem to dominate the situation completely. He seemed to be playing a part too arduous for him. Slight in stature and with a small head, he had tiny eyes graced with bushy eyebrows set beneath a narrow forehead. Thick, horn-rimmed glasses concealed still further eyes that lacked any brilliance. His hesitant smile was stopped midway, changing into a grimace.

How could a self-respecting man pledge his life in such a market? I asked myself. What debased opinion must he have of women? And this woman was my own sister. How could I allow such a degrading masquerade to take place — I who always talked about reforming society?

My sister was sitting between my mother and Sasson's father, while Sasson contemplated her from the other side of the room. I walked over to her.

"I have to talk to you," I told her abruptly.

Wanting to avoid any argument, she came docilely at the commanding tone in my voice. My grandmother, who on this solemn day was presiding over my sister's actions, agreed to my request with a mixture of surprise and anger.

"What secret is your little brother going to share with you?" she asked with a grin and a tone of false gaiety.

She stood before me. I took my sister into a corner.

"You know how much I love you," I said.

"Of course, and you know I love you too."

"If you think Sasson is ugly, you shouldn't marry him."

She lost some of her self-assurance.

"No one can force you to marry him," I went on boldly. "Don't forget that I'm here. You can count on me. I won't agree to a marriage that would be against your wishes."

Moved, she put her arms around me and kissed my cheek.

"I'll remember what you've just said as long as I live."

"You can count on me," I insisted, as though to reassure myself of my own power and authority.

"Yes, I know I can count on you. But you know that for a woman the only beauty a man possesses is in his character, his position and his mind."

Relieved, I asked for other confirmations.

"So you're becoming engaged to him of your own free will?"

"Of course. Sasson is a fine man."

Later I congratulated her, swelling out my chest, protective, mag-
nanimous. At the same time, I was haunted by a painful feeling.
Those protests of dignity were a travesty. The great joke: I,
the defender of feminine freedom? Was being a man nothing
but appearance?

TWENTY-FOUR

WHEN I WAS A CHILD, my father used to take me to the Moshi café, at the end of Bank Street, beside the river. During the day the café was a meeting place for the businessmen of that part of town, but in the evening the clientele was more varied. In summer we would sit on the terrace and my father, always alone, would follow the movement of the boats as he listened to the radio and played with his amber beads. I would walk back and forth between the backgammon players, pestering my father with my boredom and impatience to go home.

"We'll leave after the coffee has gone around five times," he would promise.

The coffee-maker would bring a dozen crockery cups, stacked inside one another. He would move them slightly so their clinking sound announced his arrival to the backgammon players. In his other hand he held the coffee pot. Behind him, a little boy collected cups from the seated customers, washed them in a bucket that he carried on a strap around his shoulder and gave them back to the coffee-maker. Together they would go around the café seven or eight times in an evening.

As soon as I started going to the cafés myself as an adult, all memories of boredom and impatience were miraculously erased.

Suddenly the cafés contained stores of unsuspected attractions. In the winter Nessim and I used to spend our evenings in the indoor cafés on Rashid Street. In the summer we naturally preferred the open-air cafés of my neighbourhood, the Battawiyeen. Haj Hammudi's café was the largest. On the day he greeted me with the nod reserved for regulars, I knew I had been admitted into the circle of the elect. Like everywhere else, most of the customers spent hours playing backgammon and checkers. Two completely different groups had made the café their headquarters: the literary and the political.

The war in Europe was over but the British troops who had protected us against Nazi invasion were still there. For years we had been waiting for the war to end. We were expecting a great release, a dramatic change in our social and political life. Everything would be possible again. Communications would be re-established and we would be in contact with the world once more. Soon we would be receiving books and newspapers from other countries and we would be free to breathe the air of other lands.

Dawn was finally visible on the horizon. We greeted it with exaltation. It would be wrong to leave our country when everything was being built. We soothed our regrets and our uneasy consciences, telling ourselves that our departure was only being delayed. Through knowledge acquired in the distant West, we would gain new instruments of combat. Doors would be opened to us when we returned and no one would be able to snatch the power that was rightly ours.

Nessim and I were part of the group which had set itself the task of building the new Iraqi culture.

Many Jews flung themselves into political combat. They were comrades-in-arms of Muslims, Christians, Armenians and Kurds. Together they were preparing for rebirth through revolution.

They haunted the same cafés that we did. We sat elbow to elbow and found ourselves on the same side of the barricade. We would divide the tasks, that was all.

But our camaraderie lasted only a few weeks. As soon as the ideological debates began, the closeness crumbled away. The political group showed intransigence and scorn when our works did not reveal sufficient proof of usefulness.

The day I learned that the war was over, I walked down Rashid Street, imagining myself already in Paris. I was reading Thibault and the silhouette of Paris, finally liberated, rose before me, the Café du Croissant where I could see the traces of the bullets that had brought down Jaurès. Iraq would be rebuilt, but first Europe had to be tamed.

Memories of the *Farhoud* were growing distant. We were united to our Muslim and Christian brothers.

At last we were going to forget our distinguishing marks, to bring down walls. We would reject any grounds for discord, refuse to assign malicious intentions to our companions. We wanted at all costs to maintain our confidence, for otherwise we would be the only losers.

Nessim and I had come to the group filled with trust but with no illusions. It was a challenge. Abandoning the most natural friendships, neglecting our classmates, cousins and neighbours, we launched ourselves into the midst of these strangers. We had deliberately crossed boundaries to join the opposite camp. As we were not going to be doctors or engineers, did we really have a choice? Our field was literature and our place had already been designated: among the Muslims.

Like other groups, the Jews gathered in cafés. In some neighbourhoods they made up the majority of the clientele. The wealthy were an exception. At first they scorned these places that were open to all, which made no distinction between the well-bred and the others. And then, the cafés were reserved for men and these people prided themselves on their modernism: their wives appeared in public with their faces uncovered and they felt only repugnance at the idea of perpetuating a custom so typically and basely Oriental.

At the cinema they rented boxes in order to shield their sisters or wives from the avid and insistent looks of solitary males who showed no embarrassment at expressing their pleasure through vulgar jokes and, when the crowds permitted it, by bottom pinching, to which the worthy women would submit in silence to avoid a public outburst.

These Jews had agreed to meet in private clubs. There were four which were distinguished from one another by the idea that the families who belonged to them thought their social status entitled them to it.

My uncle belonged to the Al Rafidayn Club. As soon as my articles began to appear in magazines and newspapers, I considered myself promoted to the status of adult. In other words, I was entitled to go out and, more important, to come home, when I pleased. I went to cafés with new friends — poets, journalists and writers who, besides being Muslims, were for the most part older than me. My mother was deeply concerned: a Jew lost among strange Muslims older than himself.

She often alluded to the grave dangers that were threatening me. My father took great pains to appear angry but he never managed to show any authority. As for my grandmother, she listed the boys in the family and the neighbourhood who had been led along the path of perdition by their evil associates; all had known a sad fate.

Sniffing the danger, my uncle was convinced that all these warnings were in vain. He knew it was impossible to restrain a boy who received a man's salary at the end of every month. And so he decided that two evenings a week, when guests were admitted, he would invite me to his Club.

There I met classmates from the Alliance. We were allowed the company of girls, or rather their presence. Until they turned twelve or thirteen, they could take part in mixed games; then they were kept in quarantine.

The men at the Club rarely played backgammon or checkers, a practice they left to the common types who frequented the cafés. They preferred chess, a more noble game, and most of all, cards, more serious because large sums of money were involved.

My uncle's sole pleasure was conversation. To the circle that surrounded him every evening, he would comment on local news and world events. He enjoyed a fine reputation for wisdom, levelheadedness and judgement. He was particularly liked for his liveliness and his inexhaustible store of anecdotes and proverbs. From time to time the card players would come and join the gathering of which he was the centre, trying with exaggerated laughter to console themselves for their unusually high losses.

Business leaders strolled from table to table, uttering cries of joy or rage according to the luck of the cards. Later when I walked past their sumptuous houses along the river, I thought of their trivial games.

At the Club, I rolled on the grass and laughed at jokes and pranks. The greatest moment of the day came at sunset when, on my uncle's instructions, the waiter brought me a chocolate ice-cream, putting an end to my impatient wait. For almost an hour I had watched him come and go, and I trembled with pleasure when I saw my uncle gesture to him.

One of my classmates, Elias, visited the Club as his uncle's guest too. In quiet voices we would take up the long discussions begun in the courtyard at school. Already we belonged to two different worlds. I believed that the joys of knowledge were sufficient in themselves and that our awakening to the world strengthened our awareness of the misfortune surrounding us. Elias was preparing for a career that would ensure him a comfortable living: medicine. He knew he had no chance of being admitted to the Faculty of Medicine at Baghdad as only two Jews were admitted each year and he had no hope of being among the chosen.

He listened with condescension as I spoke of Arabic literature. One day he told me that Baghdad's English-language newspaper, the *Iraq Times*, had accepted his literary criticism. It was as though he could now claim his revenge. He would be the first Iraqi contributor to the paper.

When I discreetly reproached him, he replied with the anticipated joy of infuriating me: "They don't want Jews in their literature."

His voluntary retrenchment, his deliberate refusal, put my own plans into question. Perhaps my projects and hopes were only illusions.

One evening, entering the large courtyard at the Club, I caught Elias by surprise. With exaggerated politeness, he was gesturing to a man who was hardly impressive in appearance. In his shorts, sandals and short-sleeved shirt, he looked like an adolescent with prematurely old features.

"That's Yaacoub Benyamine," said Elias as he raced over to me.

Benyamine was one of the most respected men in the community. An eminent lawyer, professor in the Faculty of Law, legal counsellor to numerous local and foreign firms, his name appeared on the boards of several community groups. Men and women of all ages and states invaded his office every day: parents who did not know in what direction to steer an only son, businessmen wondering how to approach a high Muslim official, broken families, brothers set against one another by an inheritance. They begged his intervention, asked his advice. Benyamine, a generous man, spread the elixir of his wisdom over this humble and powerless humanity.

His small house beside the river served as both dwelling and office. At the Club, Benyamine did not seek the pleasure of conversation, nor did he desire the excitement of gambling. As soon as he made his entrance, the waiters would ask the ping-pong players to yield the table to the dignitary. Without a word they obeyed and lined up to watch the great man in action. The most gifted players argued for the honour of sending the ball back to him.

The adventures and anecdotes, real and imaginary, that surrounded the legendary Benyamine were boundless. How many victories had he won for the Jews, how often had he saved the honour and dignity of the community? Any professor in the Faculty of Law who inadvertently made unpleasant remarks about the Jews had to virtually get on his knees and ask Benyamine's pardon, for he would threaten to abandon the students and professors in the Faculty to their miserable fate if his colleague did not make honourable amends.

He collected every document and was the definitive source of the history of the Jews in Iraq.

As Benyamine was going towards the Club office to telephone, I intercepted him.

"When are you going to publish your history of the Jews of Iraq?" I asked.

He looked at me with an amused smile, barely perceptible. I had to establish my credibility and assure him of my legitimate curiosity.

"I'm a writer myself," I said, without a hint of modesty, "and I'm interested in the past of our community."

In an affable tone, with the cordiality of one who not only takes you seriously but intends to take you into his confidence, he said, "Unfortunately we don't have a genizah, like the Jews of Cairo. Our past is virgin territory and it would take incalculable efforts to clear it. I don't have enough time to do the research."

Wanting to be recognized, to leave some traces in his memory, I told him about my articles.

"I've read some of them. I didn't think you were interested in Jewish questions."

"I'm mainly interested in literature."

"The European Jews have departed from the true spirit of our religion," he went on, staring into the distance. I was a witness rather than a participant. "We have been able to live among the Bedouins because we have managed to escape the destiny of the nomad. Even though we're in exile, we are not desert nomads but the nomads of God and we take shelter under his watchful eye, in a community."

"Like the Muslims?"

"Yes, except that for them the desert and divine breath, physical exile in the immensity of the earth and the exile of the soul in submissiveness to God, are the same thing. We don't need an exterior desert; we have learned how to carry God in our baggage. See how the Muslims cast off all their Bedouin virtues as soon as they pass through the gates of the city."

He was standing in the doorway of the office. He lingered a while, started slightly as he realized I was still there, then nodded goodbye.

THERE WAS ANOTHER SIDE, of bitterness and scorn, to the atmosphere at the Club. I was admitted into this Areopagus of the wealthy and notable, but I had to use the service door. Even this privilege I owed to my youth. There was never any possibility that my mother, father or brother could be my uncle's guest even for one evening.

Along with several sons of good families, the old boys of the Alliance, Elias founded a new club. Girls were admitted, blithely crossing steps that still separated us from the West. The girls who braved the traditions and prohibitions imposed by an overly concerned family were immune to any threat: young wives or fiancées hung from the protective arms of their men. There were some exceptions — young girls without a dowry who defied their thankless fate. Modernism and the veneer of culture which they displayed compensated for other qualities.

Elias discreetly suggested that I join the group. I declined. Nessim laughed in his face, mocking the callow youths who were trying to ape their elders.

The society we projected was breaking loose from that of our elders. An exclusively Jewish club seemed to me to be inhabited by ghosts. We had to play the game, interpret the part that an invisible director assigned to each of us; otherwise we were excluded. We could not tolerate spectators, for fear of seeing the mask fall, finding ourselves stripped of the disguise, and noticing the unbearable ridicule in the neutral eyes of the intruder. These young people prided themselves on being modern and complacently demonstrated their emancipation although they lived on the margins of society. They showed only scorn for the products of local culture, but their knowledge of western culture ended at Paul Bourget with occasional timid incursions into the writings of Anatole France. They did not know that these authors had long ago been translated into Arabic and delighted the first Muslim student who encountered them.

Already living in an imaginary Paris, my attachment to the West was too authentic to prevent me from reacting to these pitiful mannerisms with a certain haughtiness.

My passion for our own literature, rather than being weakened at the prospect of leaving, was rekindled. The image projected by our literature corresponded to that of our soul. We lived in the unformed, in the pain of gestation and the delight promised by life.

TWENTY-FIVE

*A*FTER THE LONG nightmare of the war, Europe's doors were opened to us at last. But the Iraqis intervened, presenting many obstacles to the future expatriate. From Palestine we heard sounds that weighed heavily on our lives. How long could we persist in our faith in a common homeland, in anti-colonialist solidarity, in building a new society?

Our friends from the Alliance roared with laughter every time they exchanged a few words with Nessim and me, on a street corner or outside a theatre or café. Were we blind or deliberately closing our eyes? What could we gain from our friendship with Muslims who had no influence and could not even help when we needed it?

The newspapers raged against the "Zionists" who were plotting, in obscurity and mystery, the theft of an Arab country. In the high circles of the community, calls for union resounded. We were Jews, not Zionists. Protests of patriotism, professions of nationalist faith, did not calm those who, in greater numbers every day, questioned our loyalty to the Arab nation.

The government passed a new law requiring every Jew who wanted to obtain a passport or to renew an old one to pay the authorities 1,000 or 2,000 dinars, guaranteeing their return to their native land. At first they accepted personal guarantees, waiting for the traveller's return, but it often happened that the guarantors themselves were on the point of leaving. Then the government required that the tax be paid in currency.

Through my uncle I obtained a passport before the new laws were enacted. A businessman friend of his, passport in hand and on the point of leaving himself, had assured, with many signatures, that my departure would be temporary. There was no paradox. Our lives were made impossible when the exit doors were closed in our faces.

Other boys and girls were leaving the country for good without asking any advice at the passport office. A powerful Zionist organization had been at work for several years, preparing its members for their new country. Young people formed cells which held clandestine meetings to learn to speak Hebrew as well as Zionist history and ideology. And then, discreetly, they disappeared. Schoolmates and office colleagues crossed the frontier illegally to take part in the new adventure. There were many surprises. Young bank workers, subordinate officials in the railways or the post office, shy and not resourceful, who seemed to live outside the currents that were stirring up the world and whom no one could suspect of having a personal conviction or even a political opinion, would pack their bags and go off to join the Jewish army secretly being formed in Palestine. These night travellers did not go through Syria and Jordan. They would go first to Iran, where they took the plane for the land that would be Israel.

One evening Nessim, who had not yet recovered from his consternation, told me that three students at the Alliance — Ezra, Edouard and Fathi — had fled together. Two of them had never concealed their Zionist convictions, though Ezra was known for his Communist activities. Barely three months earlier he had organized a strike of electricians, at the instigation of the clandestine Communist Party. Even though his two old friends were opposed to him, he had never stopped seeing them. He must have known they were the leaders of the Zionist organization.

Was it possible that in the secrecy of his heart Ezra had always had Zionist sympathies? Had Communism been a travesty for him or a last effort?

My mind was filled with these questions and I unburdened myself to Nessim, who knew Ezra much better than I did.

"I think Ezra has given himself over completely to Communism. I don't have any doubts about his sincerity. He was discouraged for a while when the electricians' strike didn't work, and he knew the police were after him and that he could be locked up at any moment."

"Maybe he's decided to give the police the slip."

"But the strike was over three months ago. If they wanted to arrest him, why would they wait so long?"

"He was being watched. There isn't the slightest doubt about that."

We debated the case endlessly, knowing we would never be able to clear up the mystery. Ezra's case was important to us because his departure concerned us directly. Were we all infected with the same virus? Then the Muslims' mistrust would be justified. Were we always to be their hypothetical allies, since those who fought beside the workers, who allied themselves with the nationalists, might one day turn their backs on their brothers-in-arms and disappear without a trace.

Our Muslim friends knew it was possible for the arm of power to strike them as well as us. No one was safe, and the blows fell arbitrarily according to the frequent changes of ministerial teams.

Suspicion lodged in the limpid sky of our friendships and our comradeship-in-arms. We spent whole evenings in spirited argument, unable to forget that we were no longer entirely on the same side.

One evening, when there were only a few of us at the café, Nazar accused Said of hypocrisy, selfishness and various black designs. Being a friend of both, I did not want to betray the one who was absent, and so I began to defend Said. Immediately Nazar became enraged. Voice trembling, eyes ablaze, he stared at me accusingly, and declared, "You're the last one who should be taking his side. Do you know what he said behind your back? That you're a Zionist and you would slip your insidious propaganda into the magazine if he weren't vigilant and didn't take care to correct your articles and neutralize your venom."

The stupefaction I felt at first quickly gave way to sorrow. The fine structure was crumbling. Nessim and I could feel its wounds. What was the use of talking about it? We were on the same side as we had been on the night of the *Farhoud*.

As we were about to leave, Nessim could no longer contain his distress. We were caught in a steel vise that we would never be able to unlock. Too proud to take pity on our fate, he gave free rein to his anger: "If they don't want anything to do with us, they could at least let us leave."

At Haj Hammudi's café the literary and political groups debated in their separate circles the form of the society that would soon see the light of day. We made the rounds of the tables. In the political group, the Communists seemed to be the leaders. There were more Jews, Christians, Armenians and Assyrians than in the literary groups. All minorities dreamed of a society which would accord them equality. The presence of Muslims on the front lines was their security and reassured them about the future. The Kurds made only brief appearances at such meetings. They had their own clandestine groups, their own illegal organs published in their language. They carried on a parallel activity but it was autonomous and met the others only at the top of the hierarchy and through ideology.

The Jews had only to become independent. They gave themselves unreservedly to the fraternity. The question of Palestine was growing urgent, destroying the apparent harmony of our group. We had to take a stand. The Communists, following directives from their leaders, outdid everyone with the most intransigent nationalistic slogans. It was the Jewish Communists who led the band, denouncing most vehemently the reactionary and imperialistic nature of anti-Arabic Zionism. And despite these cries from the heart, these declarations of loyalty, this pillorying of traitors and the uncommitted, the most fiercely nationalistic Jews bore the same trademark as the others. The fact that we were on the same earth as our ancestors was implicated. Every day leaders of the community gave new pledges of their Arabic orthodoxy and assured those who still wanted to pay attention to their oaths of fidelity that nothing linked them to the Zionists. They were Jews only in religion. The Communists were more vehement as they attacked the lackeys of western imperialism who were exploiting naïve religious feelings in order to hatch their wicked plot. They did not attack the Jewish religion directly because their Muslim brothers would then be suspected of atheism and of being anti-Islam, an accusation they wanted to avoid at any price.

The nationalist struggle which was being waged with great cries and vociferations was a bottomless gulf; one had to raise one's voice and heighten the tone of the invective in order to assure oneself of the audience's attention.

Then the Jewish Communists asked the Ministry of Information for authorization to publish an anti-Zionist newspaper. A praiseworthy propaganda effort that the authorities could not put down. It was the only legally published Communist organ. Soon, when exclusive anti-Zionism had proved its limits as a subject for editorials and reports, the editors decided to broaden the debate and study the real sources of Zionist fanaticism. It was only a beginning because the newspaper devoted most of its pages to imperialism, to the contradictions of capitalism and to the Soviet Union, where all discrimination had been abolished and Jews lived in harmony with all other citizens. Besides, it was the only country where anti-Semitism was considered by law to be a crime.

The Ministry of Information could no longer tolerate the Marxist vocabulary of this anti-Zionism and the paper was prohibited after a few weeks, its offices locked and the editors put under the strictest surveillance.

Zionist and anti-Zionist Jews rarely confronted each other. What was the use? All were looking for a way to escape and who could say which way was right? Besides, the Zionists could never express their arguments publicly. Leading citizens who professed a convenient anti-Zionism discovered unexpected allies among the nationalists of the Istiqlal, the party led by former Nazis. In shame and humiliation, they did their best to bring out the differences between Zionism and Judaism, hoping thereby to excuse themselves of the former. All Jews, without distinction, were hounded by petty vexations, no matter what their convictions were. Only the rich had the means to get around them. Every minister, every high official, was surrounded by intermediaries who with the minimum of discretion took advantage of fees whenever exceptional measures were violated.

In order to obtain import licences, Jewish businessmen would take a Muslim into their business, preferably someone from the military, a former minister or a retired high official whose presence would exonerate their firm from the laws of exception, the firm being declared Muslim.

TWENTY-SIX

ON THE SURFACE, life was normal. There were just as many births and weddings and they were celebrated noisily and with ululations. However, it was not hard to find the weakness and the secret wound in the broadest smiles. Joy, more ostentatious than ever, now seemed to have gone too far. People were laughing louder as though they wanted to hear the final echoes of gaiety. The simplest pleasures had a bitter taste. Each step, each gesture, might well be the last.

Then a Jewish senator, near death, decided to erect an enormous building that would house a school, a gymnasium, a stadium and a house for young people. My uncle shook his head sadly. Such naïveté made him smile. It was too late and we knew it.

"He's building for the Muslims. The Jews will never even see the walls," he said bitterly.

Henceforth there was a curious quality to any project that might result in fixing us on our native soil. Only plans for leaving seemed final. When we were waiting for our passports after the *Farhoud*, we knew that the worst was over, that we could hope for better days. That catastrophe was part of the past. Without admitting it, we hoped to stay and we clung to any ray of light in the sombre sky.

Now catastrophe was being traced against a calm horizon. It was before us, and the future concealed the worst misfortunes. Everywhere we read bad omens. We waited, trembling, for the darkest horrors that were leaving their temporary torpor.

We were careful to be discreet about our plans for fear that by unveiling them we might undo the various strands. In the café we approached obliquely the subjects that most affected all of us. We avoided any controversy that risked putting our positions and our real opinions into question. We talked freely and openly only about trifles. We often walked a tightrope, under the threat of touching the boundaries that separated us, and we tacitly sought to conceal the fact that we were Jews.

There was no lack of subjects of common interest. We kept coming back to literature and the inexhaustible subject: women and sex.

Muslims used the same word for wife and honour: *ardh*. Sensitive to anything that touched the purity of their wives, mothers or sisters, they nevertheless gave in to studied obscenities. Woman, absent from daily life, with no real presence in their emotional universe, was reduced to an abstraction. Closed away in her separate world, there was no danger that the most unspeakable vulgarities would spatter her, nor could the most ethereal lyricism move her in any way. She was carefully sheltered, protected, in the marvellous or monstrous structure that had been erected by the unbridled imagination of starving men.

The real world was the world of sex. In full bloom, greedy, joyful in the splendour of an appetite which sets aside all feelings of sin or guilt. Prostitutes were its dispensers, receptacles, an inexhaustible reservoir. They were objects, instruments for the redemption of love, mirrors reflecting to the next offended man the image of a humiliated tenderness, of a mutilated sensitivity.

As Jews we did not harvest less bitter fruits and our universe was scarcely more real. We caught glimpses of our sisters and female cousins through small openings in doors and in the corridors. That was our privilege and our superiority. When I rang Nessim's door, his sister would sometimes let me in. I would greet her timidly. She, equal to her condition, had to discourage me and act reserved. My friends and I could not indulge in bold behaviour without considering the defiled femininity of our sisters. We had seen and recognized the face of woman, the sister of our friend, and we tacitly admitted our secret weakness. Nessim refused to accept this restraint but he could not conceal his vulnerability and the force of his emotions except through bravado or an off-hand manner. As soon as he had plunged blindly into vulgarity, he would stop midway like a child caught doing something wrong. "Which do you prefer," he would ask me in a challenging voice, "breasts or bums?"

I refused to let him slip into this kind of trap. He would be the first to regret such paltry consolations. And in the most normal voice, I would answer, "Both."

"I don't. I'm an ass man."

One night an acquaintance of mine, Akram, came with his completed manuscript. We liked his poetry and sympathized with his cries of distress which were our own as well. Short, thin, dark and pimply, he looked like a patient who had left the hospital too soon. He spoke quickly, jerkily, skipping from anger to effusion. He read us his poems as he wrote them. As soon as he took a few sheets of paper out of his pocket, silence composed of respect and expectation would reign. We did not ask him about his writing because there was a danger of plunging him into profound sorrow. Often he would moan, with tears in his eyes, "I haven't written a thing, nothing of any value."

We studiously acted indifferent, thus increasing his joy when he took the great surprise from his pocket.

Akram was madly in love with Khaled's sister. He had actually spoken to her only once, almost three years earlier. She was just fourteen at the time. Since then, as soon as he approached the house and she saw him through the window, she would run to hide from his blazing eyes and warn her brother of his visit. Rashly, Akram thought that she was not insensitive to his passion. No one dared refer to it, but no one could ignore it either. We wondered whether Khaled knew about it. Probably he preferred not to notice. And if Akram had been a little bolder, he would have been forced to sacrifice his friendship. Akram could always ask for the girl's hand, but he did not even earn enough to pay for his coffee and cigarettes.

That particular evening his poem seemed to go on forever. Its soaring lyricism barely concealed his ridiculous adolescent dreams. Besides, his descriptions were as precise as they were detailed. Everything was dealt with: the mouth, the arms, the ankles, the waist. He was addressing his mistress, recalling the happy days when they had shared the same bed. We could no longer let ourselves be swayed on the rhythm of his words. We knew that he was hopelessly in love, but his eyes were not focused on the woman he was undressing, unconsciously and with determination. However, our skepticism did not please us. It was no sign of superiority. At most it marked a loss of innocence, a premature aging, for our own experiences were much like his. And like him, we had done nothing more than look at girls.

When he had finished reading, a sense of reality was restored. Never had it been so imperious. We needed women. Without transition, Akram began to describe the red-light district in Basra, which he had visited the month before while staying with his uncle. He had still not recovered from his surprise. The neighbourhood was like the one in Baghdad, the Maydane, but in the southern city the system had been perfected in a different way.

"There's a sign on every door, like the ones over a store: Madiha Ahmed, prostitute; Maziha Rashid, tenant. I went there three times during the week I was at my uncle's. I picked the cheapest ones so my money would last. There was no danger of going to the wrong door even if the lights weren't as bright as in the Maydane. You don't need a guide to find the prostitute you've chosen. All you have to do is look at the signs as though you were looking for a dentist's office on Rashid Street. The search can last a long time because there are dozens of signs. But who would complain at having to go shopping in the red-light district?"

His praise for the prostitutes of Basra was endless and he poured out details of his marvellous and surprising discoveries. Khaled interjected. The recital was beginning to irritate him. He disliked it when anyone tried to take away Baghdad's superiority.

"The Maydane is at least five times bigger," he said.

"Of course," Akram agreed, reconciled with his city. "But I still think it's ingenious to post the names on every door. You don't have to run all over before you locate the goods, and it's there for anyone to buy."

The discussion soon took another turn. Imperceptibly, we were engaging in a political debate. Nazar began to castigate the hypocrisy of the whole social system. Nessim decided to lead the debate back to where it had begun. Turning to me he said, "It's an admirable practice, putting up those signs. They say it was a former mayor of the city who had that bright idea. We won't miss the show when we go to Basra."

I did not reply. And Nessim, bitterly aware of the gap in his romantic education, exclaimed, still addressing me, "Before you go to see the red-light district in Basra, you ought to start with the one here in Baghdad."

Akram and Khaled started, and with a single gesture, they turned to me. "What's this, haven't you been to the Maydane?"

Instead of replying, I turned to Nessim and said with a shrug, "You haven't been there any more than I have."

He did not give up. Swaggering, he sighed. "It's simply that it hasn't the slightest interest for me."

"At least I have the courage to admit that it does interest me and I'm not ashamed to say I've never had a chance to go there."

For Akram and Khaled, my regret was a reminder of the duty they still had to perform. Without a moment's hesitation, Akram got up and announced, "Let's go right now."

I had no choice. Any backing down would have been considered cowardly. Fearing Nessim's haughty abstention, I attacked. "Of course you wouldn't lower yourself to go to the same place as the common people."

He sighed, shrugging his shoulders, and conceded. "I'll go with you."

I was finally going to breathe the air of this forbidden world where the laws governing our lives had not taken hold.

TWENTY-SEVEN

WE WERE IN THE Muslim part of the city. The entry to the Maydane looked out on Rashid Street. There were stores, shops and restaurants on both sides of the street. Passersby and businessmen minded their own affairs without concern for the mysteries which haunted this peaceful neighbourhood. The police stayed in their cabins, sheltered from the day-to-day world.

Nessim and I were the first to pass through the antechamber, followed by Akram and Khaled. A policeman grabbed each of us in turn, ran his hands over our thighs and chests, feeling in our pockets. It was a necessary precaution, Akram told us. And sometimes useless. Only yesterday someone had infiltrated the section, concealing his dagger from the vigilant eyes of the police. He had come to murder his sister who was dishonouring the family by selling her body.

Feeling the policeman's hand on me, I realized that this was not a simple, routine precaution but an initiation into a secret Bedouin ritual. As the policeman pressed his rough fingers against us, he was warning us that tribal laws were not in effect here.

Maydane. In popular language it was the synonym for every form of debasement, every kind of low behaviour. When anyone wanted to insult a woman, he would invoke the Maydane. It was enough to say the word with reference to a gesture or a practice and the denunciation would be relentless.

The winding streets were strewn with cafés, large and small, and the women stood on their doorsteps or behind windows which poured out light. On the benches of the cafés the *kawads*, the intermediaries, bargained with customers who took their time choosing their partners, peacefully sipping tea or a *nargileh*. It was a street of total freedom. Everywhere else women were hidden, mysterious, sheltered from our looks. Here they moved, ambulant shadows, reduced to a single organ: their sex. That which elsewhere was jealously protected, here was displayed like a banner.

As soon as we were inside, we were accosted by three prostitutes: one had only one eye, the other limped outrageously and the third was so decrepit that at first glance she seemed to be asexual. I barely had time to look at them when I felt a hand pulling on my manhood. It was the one-eyed woman. I was dumbfounded to see a woman go so directly to an unknown man. I had to shed my old beliefs and accept this complete reversal of roles. Here the women were totally nude. According to the laws of the desert, this physical nudity was naturally accompanied by moral nudity. The boundaries between what was real and what was dreamed became evanescent. Obscenity had no meaning since everything was obscene. I protected myself instinctively against such an assault and walked with my hands crossed in front of me, like armour. The blows came from another direction. Behind me, I could hear the laughter of a prostitute accompanied by her *kawad*. As they passed us, she touched me lightly and pinched my behind. Then she teased me. "Don't be scared, you aren't a girl."

And as though to warn me about the suspicions that might have fallen on me, a man with hennaed hair and reddened lips

parted the two sides of his white *dishdasha*, exposing his pro-
truding buttocks. A solid countryman, wearing the *keffiyah* and
the *akal*, pinched him as he passed. The boy burst into coarse
laughter, like a woman being tickled.

There were women everywhere. And in the blinking light of
the cafés, the men kept shop. They were the masters. They negotiated, bargained and sold.

In vain did the prostitutes exhibit their thighs and breasts,
for they could not conceal their infirmities or the ravages of time.
These were the ones who had retired from service, the leftovers.
I no longer shuddered with desire but, rather, winced at the sight
of the amputated hands, missing eyes, limping legs. I could feel
their pain in my own flesh. Hands were stretched out to me. It
was useless to protect myself. I resigned myself and abandoned
my manhood to anyone who came by. Akram stopped in front of
one of the houses.

"There it is," he said, showing us a moving shadow behind
the shutters. The shadow bent down and, recognizing Akram,
called to him. He became frantic. He was trembling with impatience, scratching himself everywhere and hopping around. He
came over to me and begged, "Lend me some money. I was here
yesterday and I haven't got a cent."

I gave it to him with a great feeling of relief. Someone was
going to perform the magic act for us and we would not have
come in vain. The only way to restore the image of femininity to
these women who had been reduced to objects was to agree to
intimacy with them, to share ourselves with them, even if only
for a few minutes. Only the onset of desire could make us forget
the mud that was spattering and choking us.

"Go for a walk and come back in fifteen minutes," Akram
ordered as he slipped inside the house.

The muddy soil gave way under our feet. Everywhere buckets of dirty water were being emptied onto the ground. The torrid sun would soon dry it. Inside a café a radio was clamouring a love song. As we moved, the streets were wrapped in darkness. We came to the end of our walk. There were few prostitutes. Soon we would retrace our steps. Two voices called to us from a barely lighted doorstep. We could almost distinguish the two women.

"So you haven't found anything," said the first, and the other reached the same conclusion.

"Come with me. You'll be satisfied. Guaranteed."

"We just came for a walk," I said, as though to apologize.

Images of this world pursued me, oppressing me for weeks. When the effect of the surprise was over, I saw nothing strange about it. These men and women were identical to the ones I met every day. We had isolated them, put them in quarantine in order to rid ourselves of our accumulated dreams and despotic desires. Often ghosts would burst out of the shadows at night, composing infernal rounds and disappearing in endless nightmares. And yet they were not phantoms, products of a fevered imagination. They were also scenes from our lives, links in the long chain of empty days and blazing nights. How many times, when desire was unbearable, had I not evoked these dozens of women, freely offered to me, images of overwhelming joy? And reality and imagination came together, changing into nightmare.

Later, every time I saw a woman on the street, I imagined her holding out her hand to the sex of the man walking past, and I relived the scenes of those jubilant streets where the odour of dirty water and urine blended with those of henna and essence of roses. I saw again all the corpses walking through a clamour of music and coarse laughter.

TWENTY-EIGHT

I WAS STILL CORRESPONDING with my French mentor, sending him my articles. As an Arabic scholar he could comment on them. He told me what books to read and frequently referred to my trip to Paris as though it were a certainty: "You will discover a love of the land which does not exist in the East and which is the indelible mark of the French peasant," he told me. He was methodically preparing me for my new life. I begged him for specific details about my immediate prospects. "Keep yourself ready," he advised me. He recommended me to the qualified authorities. The results would come soon. My departure was drawing near. I began to haunt the passport office again. I resigned from the bank and kept informed about the schedules of ships sailing between Beirut and Marseilles.

Then for long months there was silence. Not a sign of life from him in spite of my urgent letters. No, it would not happen this time.

Now my city and my house seemed to be places of exile. I talked incessantly of the hole where I was being kept prisoner.

By the end of summer I had to resign myself to what was happening. I began to look for a new job and enrolled in the Faculty of Law, for night courses.

The concern of one of the employees at the French Legation led to my getting a job at the Belgian Legation. This man, a Syrian who had become a naturalized French citizen, had defended the interests of France during the dark hours of the war. When diplomatic services were interrupted, he was his adopted country's unofficial representative. It was he who reopened the doors of the Legation when France resumed diplomatic relations with Iraq, as he waited for the arrival of the official emissary from the Quai d'Orsay.

He showed me goodwill and kindness and yet he was incomprehensibly hesitant about my planned departure.

My work at the Belgian Legation began under the best auspices. I had an excellent salary, the Belgian mission was close to the Faculty of Law and at last I was going to live in a milieu which, if not French, was at least European.

To the representative from Brussels, the Iraqis seemed to be an absurd people. I was his native guide, going with him on his first walks through the city. His reactions changed from astonishment to consternation. At every step he sighed with weariness and self-sacrifice, and cries of rage alternated with sarcastic laughter. In his eyes, Iraqi life was a tissue of bizarre and savage practices.

"No wonder the country is so backward!" he exclaimed. "Look at those men, in the middle of the day, right in the business district, who would rather drink coffee and smoke their *nargilehs* than look after their business."

I did my best to explain that the most important business was conducted right in the cafés.

"Those men stare at you morning and night. They spend most of their time counting the people going by. You don't have to look far for the real reasons for the misery in this city."

Wherever he went, dozens of eyes were levelled at him, staring from head to toe. I tried to explain that this was the lot of every foreigner, but his resentment only grew.

At the office, he set an example of the merits of work. To him, Iraqi office hours were an insult to the virtues of efficiency and seriousness. By his standards, working from eight in the morning until only two was absurd. And so at the Legation we adopted European hours, as in Brussels. We arrived at nine o'clock in the morning, and as there was no time to go home to eat at noon, the chief decided to feed us from his own kitchen, and we were deprived of our siesta.

On the first day of the new régime, the Belgian representative had a headache and he retired to the second floor which served as a residence for the diplomats. The next day, victim of colic, he went up to his room to rest. Obviously he had little resistance to the long Iraqi days, and it was not even the height of summer. On the third day, not wanting to admit defeat, he remained stoically at his desk. Early in the afternoon we found him collapsed, his head on his arms, snoring. Now or never, we had to give him a lesson and confront him with our own problems. I knocked at his door, loud enough to awaken him. He started, trying to dissimulate with an awkward smile. He blamed a sleepless night for his ill-timed nap. At the end of the afternoon, he abandoned the struggle. He announced his decision: from now on, like all the other natives, we would follow the local timetable.

TWENTY-NINE

L IVING IN A PERIOD of transition, we were caught between the past which we buried with our curses and the future which we were impatient to conquer. Career, success, status: we would have them, but later. The politicians, the wild ones, were frightened men in spite of their talent and academic success. People avoided them, mistrusted them. We, the literary ones, gave the impression of malleability. With a little savoir-faire and flexibility, with discipline and training, they could count on us.

One day I was visited by an acquaintance of my uncle who represented various English and French firms in Iraq. He offered to take me into his service, promising ideal conditions and a generous salary.

"I intend to continue my education," I said. He pointed out that after four or five years of study, my salary would not be higher than what he was offering me now.

How could I tell him that education was only a pretext? He sensed the real nature of my refusal and to sweep away any possible reluctance, he suggested that at his expense I go work for a company in France.

"For how long?" I asked, full of hope.

"Three months, four if necessary."

Paris, he felt, was not a propitious place for my apprentice-ship. I could, of course, spend a few days there before I returned.

Without hesitation, I refused. This was a mere distraction from my keen desire to live out the passion that was consuming me.

There were already some deserters and turncoats in our group. Nessim had not resisted the seduction of the immediate. For months he swore by Saroyan and Hemingway, translating their stories into Arabic, writing essays and articles about them. He dreamed of violent literature, passionate and direct. But he was impatient to be recognized for a work which he had only theoretically the desire to write.

Nazar took great care of his hair. He was tall and his abun-dant locks restored the balance which was broken by the small features of his rumpled face. With studied gestures he tried to make up for a lack of authority and a simpering manner. He used cigarettes to exhibit his masculine traits.

He wrote a story that bowled us over. He called it "We Are Twenty." He expressed what all of us felt yet dared not declare. Our country was on the threshold of great upheaval and we were debating our own future with no thought about building it. At twenty, Nazar said, Mozart was a recognized genius, Keats a great poet and Gibran followed by enthusiastic disciples. Where were we? Full of promise, we kept postponing our entry onto the scene.

Nazar had never expressed a desire to leave. In a year he would have finished his law courses and he intended to build his nest at home.

He did not even need to wait so long. At the beginning of summer, he announced to the dismayed assembly, "I'm going to Kirkuk. I'm leaving in a week."

He had been hired by the Iraq Petroleum Company. He offered this British company all the guarantees they wanted: a young lawyer, Muslim, with an exceptional command of the English language.

And so we learned, with a hollow feeling, that literature could be reduced to a transitory, ephemeral role. Nazar would find other confirmations. Soon he would marry and leave us forever. He was our first victim.

THIRTY

ALTHOUGH ELIAS WAS caught up in his functions as secretary of the Club of Alliance graduates, he was still concerned about his future. He did not expect a scholarship from the government or any other source.

"If you want to appreciate literature, you mustn't make it a subject of academic study. You have to approach it directly, innocently."

Then he made his apology for medicine.

"To really train the mind, make it flexible and precise, scientific discipline is essential. It teaches us to reason, and we can use our logic in any area. A mind isn't serious unless it has had scientific training."

I knew he had no taste for science but he would not admit defeat. He wrote methodically to all the institutions in every city. These schools, which were preparing to receive contingents of demobilized soldiers, made exceptions only for foreigners with scholarships from their own governments or from the British Council. Unfortunately, all the Faculties of Medicine in the British Isles claimed they had not received Elias' applications.

With medicine ruled out, Elias discovered, as a last resort, the merits of political science and economics.

Imperturbable in the face of this latest abdication, I stood by my own plans. I was going to study literature. With a protective smile, Elias swept aside all my arguments: "And what will you do when you're finished?"

"I'll write."

"But you're already doing that. Why do you need diplomas?"

When school started again, Nessim did not return to his studies. He no longer made a distinction between his dreams and their realization. It was enough for him to give an appearance of reality to his most stirring projects. He was not completely lacking lucidity and he decided to postpone starting them. This gave him the illusion that the facts were obeying his own good will.

We were all waiting for a scholarship and a visa, but Nessim's fate was tied to that of the growing company. Later he would set up branches in the world's capitals. When my education was finished, I would be able to take over one of the European branches. He distributed the unreaped fruits of harvest to all his friends.

Our friendship was precious and I did not want to hasten its disintegration by doubting his plans. Distance would cause enough ravages without that. Besides, I had to believe in the reality of his plans, to count on our meeting one day in Paris, London or Milan. How could I tear myself away from my city, family and friends, except by believing that sooner or later they would join me?

In Said's attempts to obtain a scholarship, acquaintances, relatives and friends intervened. What was he going to study: painting, sculpture, literature, archaeology? He was ashamed that he was about to became a student again. Had he not already crossed the barrier, since he gave drawing lessons in a secondary school? For him as for the rest of us, education was only a pretext for going to live in Europe. In his own mind, he was already there.

One evening he invited us to his house to celebrate his birthday. Incredulous, we accepted the invitation with a smile. It would be the first time one of us had observed his birthday. Some of us did not even know the date. Carried along on the wave of enthusiasm, Said announced that he was going to celebrate his twentieth birthday. This was too much. We burst out laughing. We were all between seventeen and nineteen, and Said must have been at least twenty-three or twenty-four. Why was he being coy about his age, like a woman?

Getting to his house was an expedition. The only instructions he gave were to ask the man who had the tobacco store at the corner of the fourth street left of the Bab el Sheikh mosque.

"It won't be so complicated in Paris," Nessim teased him. "You'll just have to give the name of the street and the number of the house. In this uncivilized country of ours, we don't even have proper addresses."

Usually Said would defend our civilization and our glorious heritage if anyone evoked the false superiority of the West. But this time he did not protest.

At nightfall Nessim and I were in front of the tobacconist's. None of us was in the habit of inviting friends to his house and this was the first time we had gone to Said's. It was also the first time we had entered this part of town which was so obviously Muslim.

"Ah, you're looking for our house," said the tobacconist.

"No, it's Said's house where we have an appointment," I corrected him.

"It's the same thing," he said, laughing. "Said is my brother."

He wore the *yashmagh* and the *dishdasha*. His shop also had a traditional appearance. It was lit only with an oil lamp and crowded with different coloured bags of tobacco. On a shelf at the back there were a few rows of cigarettes. His customers were poor and must have rolled their own cigarettes.

Said's door was wide open. Two women, draped completely in black veils, were crouching in a corner of the courtyard. They asked if we were friends of Said. Without waiting for a reply, they indicated where we were to go: the *kabishkan* on the first floor. The older woman let us have a glimpse of her eyes. The second turned around as soon as we came in and showed us only her back. Neither considered it necessary to be so familiar as to say goodbye, showing us the interest they would have accorded to any stranger in the street.

We made our way to the first floor, eager to find shelter with our friends.

We had never associated Said with his family surroundings. Now he was at home. The two veiled women were his mother and sister-in-law. He would have been as surprised, and felt as out of place, in our homes. We were all isolated from our surroundings. And Said, without being ashamed of his tobacconist brother, did not even speak the same language he did.

Celebrating a birthday in such surroundings began to resemble a grotesque farce in which we were both actors and spectators.

"This is the room where I work," Said explained as soon as we came in. He thought this would justify its rudimentary furnishings. We were sitting on an iron bed.

"I don't sleep here," he went on. "My bedroom's down below. This is where I take my siesta."

Nazar, Janil and Akram, who had already arrived, sat on

the bed behind a little red wooden table. A few stools were against the wall, occupying the minuscule space on the other side of the table, which was decorated with two small bottles and a few glasses.

"I didn't buy anything except cognac and whisky," Said apologized. "I hope there aren't any *arak* drinkers here."

He went to the door. "Please excuse me for a few minutes. I'm going to tell the maids to prepare tea."

He came back with a tin of biscuits imported from England. He unwrapped it and passed the tin around. The ceremony was beginning. We were not aware of the game in which we had been invited to participate. We were imitating Europe but we would have preferred to amuse ourselves in our own way. Nessim's mind was drowsing, unable to toss off a joke that would have broken the ice. He was feeling too out of place.

We sighed with relief when we heard heavy footsteps on the stairs. Said was the first to smile.

"It's the maid bringing the tea."

Who was he fooling? We could see very well that it was his mother. Was he ashamed of her?

The cups Said had used disturbed us, for we usually drank from small glasses. This must be a European custom.

Said was full of concern and solicitude for our slightest wishes. Was he really happy or only pretending?

Were we going to be accomplices in this mock show which struck us as a degrading comedy, even a betrayal? It was no longer a game. We had become engaged in an awkward rehearsal for our future lives in Europe. Would we follow Said cheerfully down this path, pay such a high price? Must we, like him, deny our mothers and be ashamed of sleeping in a narrow iron bed?

Nazar suggested we continue the party in a café, where Said would be our guest. We leaped at the chance, and Nessim rediscovered his inexhaustible fund of jokes. We were no longer puppets in an absurd and incomprehensible ceremony.

THIRTY-ONE

O NE NIGHT AKRAM told us he had reached a grave decision: he was going to abandon poetry. But not literature.
He wanted to hear the heartbeat of his people, surprise the
masses in their everyday reality. He refused to give us any other
details, asking that we be patient until tomorrow.

The next day he came into the café with Ishaq, a deserter
from the political group. It was he who explained Akram's plan.
By way of preamble, he offered us the theory of the *engagé* writer,
branding the dreamers who were blind to the misery of their
people, deaf to its appeals.

"They are traitors who take refuge in their ivory towers to
relieve their consciences."

The new group had set itself the task of putting into practice
the theories of engagement. Ishaq had already established the
premise. He had written an article on the role of the writer
and he had only to give a demonstration that would illustrate
the accuracy of his theory. He and Akram were going to set to
work the following day. Their task was to rediscover the city
through systematic exploration. Every day they would carry out
their investigations in a particular street or neighbourhood.

They would sit in a café, speak to the people, mingle with them. The next day they would record their observations in an article which would be accepted for publication in a daily paper because Ishaq was a friend of the editor-in-chief. It was essential that a Jew and a Muslim be associated, not only for success but also for practical purposes. Each would act as interpreter for the other. Ishaq's presence in a Jewish neighbourhood was like a visa to a universe which would otherwise have been closed to Akram. The latter would be content to listen to his fellow worker's conversations with his coreligionists while Ishaq would remain silent in the Muslim groups.

We read the articles with a certain embarrassment. This exploration masked a more secret quest. Akram was growing tired of constantly rewriting the same love song. His universe, divided between prostitutes and the ideal woman, was crumbling; it no longer even had the consistency of a dream. He was painfully trying to fasten on to a real world, to living beings. He was going to the people armed with naïveté and condescension. His realism reeked of artifice. Some days we could distinguish the writing style of one or the other, Akram's lyric flights or Ishaq's heavy imagery and preciousness. Ishaq wanted to be recognized as a writer and at the same time earn his admission into the Muslim world, through an act of faith and a declaration of principles. Despite his diligence at embellishing the world which he claimed to present in all the spontaneity of discovery, he was still completely foreign to it. He did not bother with scruples as soon as he could make the others, and himself, believe that he had a legitimate place in this society.

THIRTY-TWO

A TELEPHONE CALL from the French Legation announcing that I had been awarded a scholarship by the French government did not bring the joy I had anticipated for so long. I had been so eager for this news that I had finally exhausted its true consequences, having already integrated it into a prolonged and manifold dream. I had lived this moment so many times in my imagination that it was already located in a past whose memory I now evoked.

The next day I went to have a visa added to my passport. The Syrian official told me that he intended to leave too, to leave Iraq and the diplomatic service. He was going to join a sister in the United States, and would spend his vacations in France.

He held my hand in his for a long time, congratulating me. He belonged to the two worlds which in my mind resembled two waves. No one could understand my happiness and apprehension better than this Syrian, who spoke Arabic. He had succeeded in making the difficult union between his origins and his adopted country; and in my eyes he incarnated the great ideas of France. Yet, was he really inspired by the French spirit of which he was the spokesman? How could he then explain his intention to live in America? I assumed the decision was his wife's, whom I considered to be as uncultivated as a Bedouin despite her lipstick and nail polish.

"I can tell you now that I was opposed to giving you this scholarship," he said in his calm, warm voice.

I don't know if I turned red or white with consternation.

"That surprises you, and I understand. Do you know why the French government gives those scholarships to foreign students?"

"Yes, of course I know."

But I could not follow him. First of all, did I really know why? And then, what was the use of arguing with a man whom I was suddenly seeing with an unexpected face? My pain was real, like the pain of a hurt child.

"France wants to retain its influence in the Middle East. She has to train allies to defend her in the future. You're a Jew. You're going to study in France. You'll be successful and you won't come back. A Muslim, the son of a minister or a senior official, wouldn't have that choice. He would have to come home. He would spend most of his time in Paris cafés or chasing girls, but when he came home he would have influence in his own milieu. Out of gratitude, he would use that influence to defend the interests of France."

Here I was before a man whom I had always taken for an ally and a friend, who was now revealing, without the least embarrassment, his opposition to my departure. He was the first Frenchman I had caught in the act of betrayal. I reassured myself by thinking that, after all, he was only superficially French.

And yet he was right. How could I honestly contradict him? If the choice had fallen to me, in spite of everything I owed my luck more to chance than merit. My responsibility was nonetheless a heavy one, and I would have to take as much from it as I could.

THIRTY-THREE

THE SAME DEBATES were going on in the cafés, but weariness had set in. We were going around in circles and the objections we raised were only for form. We were already somewhere else, weighing the various aspects of Iraqi problems out of duty, afraid to break the spell of unity. No one wanted to take it upon himself to put an end to a period of our lives. We clung without conviction to friendships that were crumbling away in silence.

Before a week had passed, the authorities had designated one of us for the much-wanted privilege of leaving. Plans were becoming more specific. Akram and Said, with their scholarships, were going to further their knowledge in Paris. They would enroll at the Beaux-Arts. Hussein and Fahmi, who had also won scholarships, were going to the United States. Zaki had been hired by the Ministry of Foreign Affairs and he was going to work at the Iraqi Embassy in London. We assured him of our friendship and mournfully swore to be faithful. We would meet in the great capitals of the world, happy to confront one another. Hussein and Fahmi were going to spend their summer holidays in Europe. We would take turns going to visit Zaki in London. My first task in Paris would be to find a room for Said.

"Be sure not to tell anybody that I'm going to study fine arts," he asked me. "It would be very embarrassing since I'm already a teacher."

Of all the scholarship winners, I was the only one who had not had to ask cousins or ministers to intervene. Of course, the Iraqi government proved to be more generous than the French government and my friends' scholarships were four times as large as mine. But they had promised to work for the state when they returned.

I had not signed any papers or made any promises. By saturating me with the French mentality, they expected that I would later become its defender.

We prepared an accounting of our past. It was only a way to dream about the future. Together we would erect the new structure, and Iraqi culture would be the fruit of our collective engagement. Promises poured from our lips, ran together, burst out in joy. They were not born of the misery of our existence or our impatience. They were an extension of real riches, which were now within our grasp, available to us tomorrow. We would not forget Iraqi literature as we strolled through the Latin Quarter or along the bridges across the Seine. We would speak of it to beautiful French women and eminent French men. It would be our calling card and we would produce it proudly.

We would have so much to say, so much to reveal, that we would not be able to keep silent. Said dreamed of turning our magazine into a European or even a world publication. It would open its pages to all the Arabic intellectuals who were scattered through western universities.

We knew there was little time for final words of advice, our last declarations of loyalty to our youth. It was as though we were waiting for a train in a station and, having exhausted all our words, all our phrases, we were spending the last fifteen minutes in savage jokes.

In fact, we were no longer thinking about literature or even about Iraq. We were about to separate and each of us would follow his own destiny. We would meet again under other skies, in other circumstances, and each of us would have been transformed.

The situation of the Jews was becoming increasingly threatened every day. The government took steps to control their movements. The exit door was being closed more and more firmly. No doubt there was too much corruption in high places to prevent the wealthiest Jews from escaping the nets that were being held out for them. Now these wealthy Jews were paying the price.

Elsewhere, there were more and more escapes and clandestine departures. The Jewish state would soon be born; and in their heart of hearts, all Iraqi Jews were rejoicing, hoping to be witnesses and builders of the great event. They were rigorously discreet. The slightest sign of sympathy would bring severe punishment. The police put the same label on everyone. Behind bars, Zionists and Communists, fierce adversaries, were accused of the same crime: Communistic Zionism.

"Do everything you can to leave as soon as possible," I told Nessim.

"Yes, you're right. Otherwise it will be too late."

THIRTY-FOUR

WHEN THE DAY CAME for me to leave, a *nairn* was waiting for us at the bus station. We would cross the desert and the next day I would be in Beirut, the first step on the road to the West. A few days more and I would be on board ship, sailing for Marseilles.

My whole family was there. The pain of separation was mixed with relief at leaving these walls which were being covered with shadows. I was the first to leave. They were all thinking it without daring to say so.

My grandmother was lavish with advice. I must not skip meals; pork would make me sick; fruits must be washed before they are eaten. My mother barely spoke. I recognized myself in her. We avoided looking at one another.

Nessim was alone, a little embarrassed. He was not a member of the family but everyone knew that he was, to a great extent, my family.

These faces looking at me, moving away from me, which I saw through the window of the bus — they were Iraq. All that remained of it for me. And I hoped I would be able to take away forever, within myself, its last reflection. It had to be so. In that way my childhood would be preserved. I would enter the new world without cutting off a privileged part of it, without dispersing my dreams and memories.

The bus was already moving along the dirt road. The sand was enclosing us, extending a curtain, cutting us off from the city which moved farther away in a fog that was ominous and dark. The road was strewn with stones which skipped into the air as the tires squealed over them. Through the tears that poured down my cheeks, I could glimpse the howling dogs that were pursuing us. Now I did not have to throw stones to get rid of them, to protect myself from them.

ABOUT THE AUTHOR

N AIM KATTAN, Order of Canada, was born in Baghdad in 1928. He studied at the Alliance Israélite Universelle School and the Law College in Baghdad and, on a French government scholarship, at the Sorbonne in Paris. In 1954 he immigrated to Canada where he founded the *Bulletin du Cercle Juif*, of which he was editor-in-chief until 1967. He has written for radio and television and has published 32 books of poetry, essays and fiction. His work has been translated widely; in English, his best-known books are *Farewell, Babylon* and the award-winning essay collection *Theatre and Reality*.

Kattan has received many honours, including the France–Canada Prize; the 2004 Prix Athanase, Quebec's highest literary award; and France's prestigious Légion d'Honneur. He taught at Laval University, is a literary critic at *Le Devoir* and was head of the Writing and Publication Section of the Canada Council for 25 years. Kattan has lived in Montreal since 1954.

SHEILA FISCHMAN, Order of Canada, is one of Canada's foremost translators and has won many prizes, including the Governor General's Award.